Discovering American Culture

Discovering American Culture

Cheryl L. Delk

Ann Arbor
THE UNIVERSITY OF MICHIGAN PRESS

Series Introduction

Content-based instruction (CBI) is the integration of content and language learning. **Alliance: The Michigan State University Textbook Series of Theme-Based Content Instruction for ESL/EFL** is designed principally for postsecondary programs in English as a second/foreign language, though some books are appropriate for secondary programs as well. **Alliance** is the first series to allow programs to experiment with content-based language instruction without the demands of teachers' time and effort in developing materials. It also offers a wide selection of topics from which both teachers and students can choose.

The rationale for a content-based approach to language instruction comes from the claim that interesting and relevant material increases motivation and promotes effective language learning. CBI also adheres to the pedagogical principle that teaching should build on the previous subject matter *and* second language knowledge of the learner, while taking into account the eventual uses the learners will make of the second or foreign language. Finally, with a content-based approach, students will grow in not one but three areas: second language acquisition, content knowledge, and cognitive development.

Three models of CBI at the postsecondary levels exist: theme-based, sheltered, and adjunct courses. The **Alliance** series utilizes a theme-based approach in which language skills, grammar, vocabulary, and cognitive skills are integrated into the study of one particular subject area. This model is advantageous in that it can be implemented in any postsecondary program and can be taught at all proficiency levels. Sheltered and adjunct courses, on the other hand, are limited to university settings with high-intermediate to advanced level students. The theme-based approach is also preferable for this series as it is the only approach that has as its principal goal the improvement of language competence rather than mastery of subject material.

Unique Features of the Series

All the textbooks have been piloted in the classroom by teachers other than the author. Because content-based instruction is a relatively new area of language teaching, our goal is to produce textbooks that are accessible to those teachers who have a great deal of experience with CBI and to those who have little or no experience. By piloting the textbooks with different teachers, we confirmed that people unfamiliar with the topic were able to teach the material easily. One teacher who taught one of the texts said "I was hesitant at first because it has been many years since I studied this subject myself, but my fears were unfounded." This piloting also allowed the authors to receive feedback on which activities worked and which didn't work to determine whether or not the material was appropriate for the level, and to check for any "loopholes" in the textbook.

 The teacher's manual provides detailed explanations for those who may want more guidance for teaching the course. Detailed explanations and information for teaching the materials are in the teacher's manuals. Teachers can use or not use the information, depending on their experience, needs, and desires.

 Each chapter in the student books states the content objectives, while teachers are provided with both content and language objectives in the teacher's manual. We expect that there is a range in teachers' philosophies toward CBI. Some teachers may accept wholly the idea that there should be no overt instruction of language and that students will naturally acquire the language through the content. Some, however, may feel that overt language instruction is necessary. By restricting the language objectives to the teacher's manual, teachers have the option to share them with their students or use them only as information to guide their teaching. The omission of the language objectives from the student's book also allows teachers to further develop any material and not feel obligated to cover "specified" language objectives.

 Explanations of language items are clearly shown in "language boxes." Any detailed language point is explained in "language boxes." These boxes give teachers the option to cover the material in class or to leave the information as reference for students to use on their own, depending on their philosophy toward CBI. The information in the language boxes also saves valuable time since teachers do not have to find the supporting language explanations from other textbooks.

Each book is devoted entirely to one particular content that builds on the students' previous learning experiences. This type of in-depth coverage allows topic-related vocabulary and concepts to be continuously recycled, thus increasing the students' knowledge of the content and language. Students will benefit from the coherence provided by an integrated skills approach with one unifying topical content.

The interests and needs of the learners are considered in the choice of topics. Our experience has shown that students have a wide variety of interests, some enjoying courses that are "entertainment" focused, such as music or film, while others prefer a more "academic" focus, such as American government or media. We have developed books that present different choices and are immediately relevant to and usable in a student's daily life.

Several choices of topics exist for the beginner, intermediate, and advanced levels. As the student population varies from term to term, so will their needs and interests. Having more than one book to choose from at each level lets students choose the topics of special interest to them. Teachers can also choose topics they are comfortable with or interested in teaching.

Authentic materials are used whenever possible. One of the goals of CBI is to use original text that was created for a purpose other than language teaching. The structure, function, and discourse features in these materials then dictate what language is to be taught. While much of the information was kept in its original form, some of the authentic texts were adapted to match the language ability of the audience.

Content material is supplemented with activities that assist students in comprehension. The material in each book has been carefully analyzed to determine those language skills that will assist the students in comprehending the information. Activities have then been developed, and any necessary language explanations to accomplish this goal have been included.

Language items are presented in an inductive format. This format encourages students to generate for themselves how or why a particular form is used. This "active" discovery helps students retain the information more successfully.

Format of the Books

Each book in the **Alliance** series follows the same format except in the Vocabulary Development section, present in some books, but not in others. This format is as follows:

Opening Activity: Each chapter opens with some sort of activity that will get the students thinking about the topic of the chapter. This opening activity may be as simple as a picture or may involve a detailed activity. Its purpose is not to master the content described but simply to raise the students' awareness of the topic.

A Look Behind/A Look Ahead: This section contains a brief review of the previous chapter and an overview of what the students will study in the current chapter.

To the Student: Each chapter lists the content objectives, and students are encouraged to read these before studying the chapter as a preview. They should also go over the objectives again at the end of the chapter to check for comprehension.

Vocabulary Development: Some of the texts include a section on vocabulary development so that the students can have a list of important vocabulary words as well as learn various strategies for developing that vocabulary.

Content Heading: The chapter is then divided into content areas marked with roman numerals. Within that content area, activities (labeled A, B, C, etc.) help students comprehend the material.

Series Acknowledgments

There are many people we need to thank for their help in making this series a reality. Most important, the authors deserve our gratitude for their dedication, insight, and cooperation toward the project despite their busy professional demands. We are also indebted to the entire staff at the English Language Center of Michigan State University. Whether or not they were directly involved, everyone was willing to adjust schedules to accommodate and support the needs of the project. From our original meeting, Mary Erwin, our project editor at the University of Michigan Press, has been our major supporter, urging, pushing, and cajoling us to meet deadlines. Her belief in this project has ultimately allowed these materials to see the light of day. In addition, we would like to thank Chris Milton along with the entire staff at the University of Michigan Press for working so hard to produce high-quality manuscripts in such a quick turnaround time. Finally, a special thanks goes to Peter Shaw of the Monterey Institute, who initially envisioned this project.

We are aware that there are still many theoretical and practical issues left to be resolved surrounding content-based instruction. We hope the **Alliance** series will make some inroads toward the resolution of some of the issues and lead to a better acceptance of this approach to language teaching.

Susan Gass—Project Coordinator
Amy Tickle—Series Editor

Author Acknowledgments

The energy and enthusiasm that it takes to write a book comes from many different sources. The series editor, Amy Tickle, helped motivate me, and I am thankful for her guidance and friendship throughout this project. Armenia Howard and Pat Walters piloted the course and gave me helpful feedback. I also appreciate the feedback from my reviewers. Finally, I would like to thank my family, former and current colleagues, and my old and new friends who all listened to my ideas and supported me during the whole process.

Cheryl L. Delk
Western Michigan University

Acknowledgments

Grateful acknowledgment is made to the following persons, publishers, publications, and university for permission to use photographs and to reprint previously published materials.

Britt Arrak for photograph of three students talking.
Connie Bashaw for photograph of Bashaw couple.
Connie Bashaw for photograph of gesture, "Stop."
Jean-Francois Berset for photograph of gesture, "I Forgot."
Borden, Inc. for permission to reprint coupon for Eagle® Brand or Eagle® Brand Low Fat Sweetened Condensed Milk.
Lewis Buell for photograph of Timber Ridge Sports.
Pam Chamberlin for photograph of Chamberlin family.
Cheryl L. Delk for photograph of Delk family.
Josh Delk for photograph of gesture, "That's Great."
Ryan Delk for photograph of gesture, "I Don't Know."
Detroit News for excerpt from "Making Teamwork Work," by Angelo B. Henderson, *Detroit News*, September 5, 1994, "Discovery" section.
Patricia Thomas De Young for photograph of MacKenzies'.
Carol A. Frazee for photograph of two women talking.
Gannett News Service for "Actions Speak Louder than Words," by Carla Wheeler and Carla A. Clarkson, and for accompanying graphic, "Silent Messages," in *Lansing State Journal*, July 22, 1993, "Today" section.
Thomas Ivan Golba for photograph of three students talking.
Hormel Foods Corporation for permission to reprint coupon for SPAM® Luncheon Meat.

Andrea Hubka for photograph of customer and cashier talking.

Hunt-Wesson, Inc. for permission to reprint coupon for Swiss Miss® Hot Cocoa.

Stephen D. Jacobson for photograph of Gales True Value Hardware.

Johnson & Johnson for permission to reprint coupon for Johnson's *baby*® shampoo.

Toru Kitaguchi for photograph of gesture, "Good Luck."

Carol E. Kubota for family photograph.

Jimmy Lenfield for photograph of three students talking.

Ruth Ann Mosher for photograph of two women talking.

Procter & Gamble Company for permission to reprint coupons for Bold® Powder or Liquid Detergent, Ivory® Dishwashing Liquid, and Head and Shoulders® shampoo.

Matt Quartz for photograph of Sears Junior Department.

Morella Ramirez for photograph of gesture, "Come Here."

Random House, Inc. for permission to reprint p. 647 and the "enroll" entry from *The Random House Unabridged Dictionary*, 2d ed.

Stephanie Reimink for photograph of customer and cashier talking.

Darryl A. Salisbury for photograph of Darryl and Shona Salisbury.

Charles P. Schafer for photograph of Schafer's Flowers.

Susan Fay Schewe for photograph of Westside Appliance.

Kimberly Smith for photograph of Amberlee Smith and Kimberly Smith.

Kimberly Smith for photograph of gesture, "Okay."

Marilyn G. Van Hare for photograph of gesture, "Can't Hear."

Western Michigan University for permission to reprint a page of the Anthropology section of the *Fall 1995 Directory of Classes*.

Western Michigan University for permission to reprint the Alpha Program section of the *1993–1995 Western Michigan University Undergraduate Catalog.*

Audrey Wierenga for photograph of Karen Sanborn, Audrey Wierenga, and Alex.

Cynia Zerba for photograph of Rite-Aid Pharmacy.

Every effort has been made to trace the ownership of all copyrighted material in this book and to obtain permission for its use.

To the Student

Learning to understand a culture very different from your own is a difficult task. Most of us usually do not think of ourselves as having values that are different from other cultures. As you continue studying English, you will see that language and culture are closely linked. This book will help you learn how to talk about another culture and then introduce you to aspects of the culture that most Americans share.

Lessons in this book will help you

- understand American culture in terms of values, behavior, and beliefs;
- identify dominant American values and their role in American society;
- comprehend different aspects of the patterns of living among Americans.

Each unit, chapter, and lesson has been designed to help you improve your English skills. There is a focus in this book on improving your listening and reading comprehension as well as your ability to speak. By studying English while studying about American culture, you will have greater opportunities for learning.

Contents

Chapter 1

Taking Off:
A First Look at Culture

Look at the following list of items. Which of the following words do you associate with the word *culture?*

art	family	communication	music
money	politics	education	food
television	sports	history	literature

To the Student

After completing this chapter, you will be able to

1. recognize the association between anthropology and culture;
2. discuss what culture means in terms of the beliefs, behavior, and values of a society;
3. understand the importance of avoiding stereotypes;
4. differentiate between various cultural values;
5. understand the basis of cultural values.

After completing this chapter, return to this page and assess your own achievement in reaching these objectives.

Vocabulary Development

The following list contains some concepts from this chapter that are important for you to understand. Go through this list and put a check (√) next to the words you know. When you are finished with the chapter, return to this list and make sure you can put a check next to all of the words. There is also room to list any additional words you have learned.

anthropology	____	ethnography	____
generalization	____	stereotype	____
complicated	____	outgoing	____
ethnic	____	diverse	____
big-C culture	____	little-c culture	____
linguistics	____	ancestor	____
archaeology	____	transform	____
judgment	____	evolve	____
context	____	participant	____
observer	____	custom	____
aggressive	____	dialect	____
individualism	____	cooperation	____
informality	____	formality	____
tradition	____	equality	____
competition	____	materialism	____
practicality	____	privacy	____
progress	____	directness	____

Other:

_____   _____

_____   _____

I. Who Studies Culture?

A. Look at the different types of scientists. Which type do you think studies the behaviors of people?

chemist   biologist   anthropologist   physicist

B. The following words are found in the first reading. Match the words with their definitions. Place the letter of the definition in the space next to the word.

1. __ ancestor   a. situation; environment

2. __ custom   b. develop gradually (little by little)

3. __ context   c. change

4. __ participant   d. someone who takes part or shares in something

5. __ observation   e. a person from whom others are descended

6. __ transform   f. action of watching carefully; noticing

7. __ evolve   g. complex; difficult

8. __ complicated   h. acts or practices common to a particular group of people

C. Read the following passage.

Many different types of scientists study human beings, but there is a special group of scientists who seem to have the most complicated job of all. These scientists are called anthropologists, and they are people who try to understand human behavior. The word "anthropology" comes from two Greek words. *Anthropos* means humankind and *logos* means word or study. Thus, anthropology is a science that can be compared in some ways with other fields of study such as sociology, psychology, political science, economics, and linguistics. Anthropologists examine the development of the human race by studying our physical characteristics, languages, customs, traditions, and cultural, political, economic, and social institutions.

Anthropology has several different branches: physical anthropology, archaeology, linguistic anthropology, and cultural anthropology. Physical anthropologists try to understand how humans have evolved from their ancestors over the last few million years. They are very similar to modern biologists who study humans. Physical anthropologists, however, study the human body of the past. Archaeologists examine different forms of social organization by looking at how humans lived. They examine how humans lived based on the remains of the houses and objects that humans have left behind. Linguists involved in the field of anthropology are interested in comparing different language forms as well as different uses of language in different contexts. Cultural anthropologists study human behavior and compare different cultures. They usually work in the form of participant observation—they live with the people whom they study for a period of time. Cultural anthropologists who record and analyze data from their participant observations are called ethnographers.

Your participation in this course will transform you into a sort of cultural anthropologist as you learn about a society that practices customs different from your own. If you are studying English in the United States, then you will be working like an ethnographer as you participate in the culture. You will be continuously comparing your culture with American culture as you see how several parts of Americans' lives fit into a way of life as a whole.

D. Answer the questions about the preceding reading passage.

1. What do anthropologists try to understand?

2. What do anthropologists study in order to understand humans?

3. What are the different branches of anthropology?

4. Which type of anthropologist studies customs?

5. Which type of anthropologist studies languages of different cultures?

6. Who observes people as a participant in the culture?

E. Fill in the missing parts of the following diagram, which outlines the field of anthropology. Use the list of words to fill in the different branches and possible subjects of different types of anthropologists.

Physical Anthropology   religions   storytelling
Cultural Anthropology   houses   human skeletons

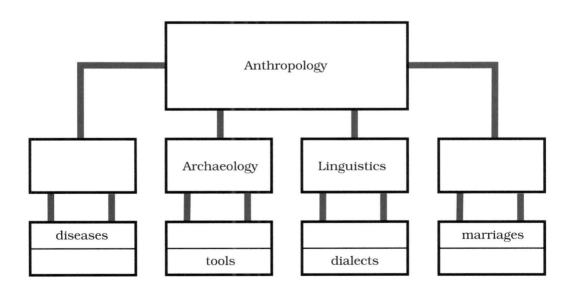

II. Different Views of Learning Culture

A. The title of the next passage you will read is "Big-C and Little-c Culture." What do you think might be some differences between big-C and little-c cultures? Think about the answers to this question as you read the next passage about the history of culture learning in foreign language teaching.

"BIG-C" AND "LITTLE-c" CULTURE

Before the 1960s, many foreign language teachers and their students believed that the main reason for learning a foreign language was to know about the history and arts of a particular culture. Because of this narrow viewpoint, learning about a foreign culture occurred only at high levels of language proficiency, only after students were able to read texts in the second language. At this level, music, literature, art, history, architecture, etc. were considered the primary focus. This type of culture learning is referred to by many researchers as big-C culture.

During the 1960s, however, communication became the goal of language learning, and teachers started to emphasize the anthropological aspects of culture. Nelson Brooks, a researcher in foreign language learning, believes that the study of culture goes beyond artistic expression (e.g., literature and art). He concentrates on the personal side of culture—"the distinctive life-way of a people." He once said, "This aspect of culture is absolutely basic to an understanding of what makes us what we are." If students concentrate on the everyday patterns of living of people in a particular culture, students can learn language and culture simultaneously. This type of culture learning is referred to as little-c culture, and most teachers today believe that it can be introduced to students at all levels of language learning.

B. Now, look back at the list of items at the beginning of the chapter (directly before the "To the Student" section) and decide which ones would be considered aspects of big-C culture and which ones would be parts of little-c culture ("patterns of living"). Label big-C items with a "C" and little-c items with a "c." It is important to keep in mind that this list is not complete and there may be some items that you believe are both big-C and little-c aspects.

Reading adapted from Nelson Brooks, "The Analysis of Familiar Cultures," *The Cultural Revolution*, ed. Robert C. Lafayette (Skokie, IL: National Textbook Company, 1975).

III. Generalizations and Stereotypes

A. Is it possible to characterize an American in just a few words? Using only three adjectives, try to describe an American. Compare your list with other students in class. Did you choose any of the same words as anyone else in your class?

1. _____

2. _____

3. _____

B. Listen to the following famous tale. Fill in the blanks with the words that you hear.

THE BLIND MEN AND THE ELEPHANT

Six blind men and a young _____ went into a forest to

find _____ elephant. Obviously, none of the blind men

_____ ever seen one, but they wanted _____ find

out what an elephant was like. They did _____ really

know what to expect. The young child directed the _____

to where an elephant was standing.

The first _____ ran into the side of the elephant and

said, "_____ elephant is like a wall."

The second man _____ the tusk of the elephant and

said, "This elephant is _____ a spear."

The third man _____ the trunk of the elephant with

his hands and _____, "The elephant is like a snake."

The fourth man _____ the elephant's ear and said, "This elephant is like _____ fan."

The fifth man reached out _____ hand and felt the elephant's knee and said, "It's like a _____."

The sixth man grabbed onto _____ tail and said, "This elephant is a rope."

Each of the blind men _____ that his judgment was correct. In fact, the _____ argued for years, insisting that their personal opinion was the right one.

C. Now reread the tale. What do you think the message is?

D. Look back at your list of three adjectives that you chose to describe an American. Do you believe that it is possible to describe an American using only three words? three hundred words? three thousand words?

E. Think of two statements that you believe describe Americans. Write those statements here and compare them with other students in the class.

1. _____

2. _____

F. Do you think that these statements are true about *all* Americans? Read the following passage and decide whether your statements are stereotypes or facts.

STEREOTYPES

When we observe other people, we often form opinions about their values and behavior. As you study the material in this textbook, you will often be asked to compare your culture with American culture, and it will be very natural for you to use your own culture as a basis of comparison. You will be considering why *you* act the way you do in certain situations, and you will also start considering why *Americans* act the way they do in certain situations. You will soon understand how important it is to avoid stereotyping.

A stereotype is a belief about another person or group of people. Stereotypes are usually oversimplified descriptions based on only one or two characteristics, and even though they can seem either favorable or unfavorable, stereotypes about national groups are often insulting. People often stereotype others based on images they have seen or heard in movies, on television, or from other people. They may judge others because of differences in ethnic, political, economic, or religious backgrounds. During your study of American culture, it is very important that you do not use stereotypes to describe Americans. Therefore, if you have seen several Americans acting a certain way and you assume that *all* people from that group *always* act like that, then you are stereotyping.

You will also be learning several facts about Americans and the culture. Facts are supported by research that uses ways of measuring things. These facts will help you avoid stereotyping people and will help you to better understand the American lifestyle.

G. In your own words, write a definition for *stereotype* and *fact.*

    1. stereotype

    2. fact

H. Read the following sentences and decide whether each one is a stereotype (S) or fact (F).

    1. _____   Americans eat too many hamburgers and hot dogs.

    2. _____   33% of all Americans are overweight.

    3. _____   Young Americans leave their parents' home at age 18.

    4. _____   Americans eat too many candy bars.

    5. _____   According to the U.S. Department of Commerce, 99% of American kindergarten teachers are female.

    6. _____   Hispanic-Americans include people with Spanish, Mexican, or Latin American ethnic origins.

I. Look at the sentence that follows. Is this sentence a stereotype? Why or why not?

Many Americans like McDonald's.

Qualifiers

Certain words are used in English to indicate that the statement is true most of the time, but not always. These are called *qualifiers*.

generally speaking	it is often the case
generally	frequently
often	perhaps
may	many

J. Rewrite the following sentences, changing them from stereotypes to general statements, using a qualifier from the language box above.

Example:

"Americans are always too busy." (stereotype)
"Americans are *often* very busy." (general statement)

1. All Americans go to baseball games during their lifetimes.

   _____

2. American people eat dinner in the late afternoon.

   _____

3. Americans eat too much junk food every day.

   _____

4. Americans smile at people they don't even know.

   _____

K. Following is a list of adjectives that are sometimes used to describe people. With a partner, think of an antonym (a word that means the opposite) for each given word.

Example:

    cheap   <u>expensive</u>

1. tall   _____

2. outgoing   _____

3. private   _____

4. helpful   _____

5. aggressive   _____

6. independent   _____

7. quiet   _____

8. hard-working   _____

L. Now, write sentences comparing Americans with people from your culture using the adjectives. Remember to use a qualifier to avoid stereotyping. Refer to the language box on comparatives on page 13.

Example:

Generally speaking, American cars are much cheaper than cars in my country.

1. _____

2. _____

3. _____

4. _____

5. _____

6. _____

7. _____

8. _____

Comparatives

When we want to compare two things using adjectives or adverbs, which is often done when we are making generalizations, we use comparative forms. For example, look at the following sentence:

In general, American cars are *larger* than cars in my country.

To form the comparative for *one-syllable* adjectives or *two-syllable* adjectives ending in *-y* add *-er* to the regular form.

cheap / cheaper   lazy / lazier
long / longer   easy / easier

To form the comparative for longer adjectives and adverbs that end with *-ly*, add the word *more* before the adjective or adverb.

quickly / more quickly   peaceful / more peaceful
loud / more loudly   carefully / more carefully

A small group of fairly common adjectives and adverbs form their comparatives in irregular ways:

good / better   bad / worse
many / more   much / more
some / more   little / less or littler
well / better   badly / worse

IV. How to Talk about Culture

Now that we have looked at stereotypes and the dangers of overgeneralizing, we can focus on how to express our opinions more effectively. Expressing your opinion is not always easy to do, especially when you are surrounded by other students. Throughout this course, however, you will often be asked your opinion about your own culture and American culture.

A. Read the following conversation.

> *Bill:* I rented the video *Jurassic Park* yesterday. I think that it's one of the worst movies I've ever seen!
>
> *Juan:* I couldn't agree more! I rented the video a couple weeks ago, and I really didn't like it.
>
> *Carlos:* You both have a right to your opinion, but if you ask me, *Jurassic Park* is one of those movies that you should see in a movie theater. I thought the special effects were great. The technology used to make that movie was very advanced. The point I'm making is that action movies are not as good on video as on the big movie screens with stereo sound.
>
> *Bill:* You could be right, but don't you think the acting was bad too?
>
> *Juan:* You can say that again!
>
> *Carlos:* Are you kidding? You have to remember that the actors had to imagine they were surrounded by dinosaurs that were created by computers.
>
> *Bill:* Well, I respect your opinion. Maybe I do have to see it on a big movie screen instead of on my television.

B. Reread the conversation and underline all the phrases that express opinion, agreement, and disagreement. Which phrases that express disagreement are direct? Which phrases are indirect?

Expressing Opinions

Here are some different expressions that can be used to let a person know your opinion of a topic.

—The point I'm making is . . .   —In my opinion . . .
—I believe . . .   —I think that . . .
—I feel that . . .   —As I see it . . .
—If you ask me . . .   —Personally, I think . . .

Agreeing

Agreeing with someone is a lot easier than disagreeing. Americans use several different expressions.

—I couldn't agree more!
—How true!
—You're exactly right!
—You can say that again!
—For sure!

—Absolutely!
—That's exactly what I was thinking!
—Definitely!
—You bet!
—I'll say!

Disagreeing

Disagreeing with someone is usually more difficult. You have to be aware of the relationship between you and the person with whom you are disagreeing. There are both direct and indirect expressions.

—You've got to be joking/kidding!
—I disagree with what you are saying.
—I don't see it that way.
—Are you crazy?

—I don't think so.

—Don't make me laugh!
—I respect your opinion, but . . .

—Don't be ridiculous!
—Well, you have a right to your opinion, but . . .
—You could be right, but don't you think that . . . ?

C. Reread the expressions used to disagree in the preceding language box. Decide which ones are direct and which are indirect. Where do you think each expression would go on the direct-indirect scale below?

1   2   3   4   5   6   7   8
Direct   Indirect

Are you crazy?

D. With a partner, go back to the conversation in Activity A on page 14. Replace the phrases of opinions, agreement, and disagreement with other expressions from the language box on pages 14–15.

E. Here are some opinions. Disagree with them in two ways: first, very directly, and then, soften the disagreement by making it more indirect. Remember to support your disagreement with a reason.

Example:

Don't you think that Tom Cruise is a good actor?

(directly)   You must be joking! All of his movies are the same!
(indirectly) Well, you have a right to your opinion, but I don't think he's very talented.

1. Personally, I think American food is really good.

   a.

   b.

2. In my opinion, traveling to other countries is a waste of money.

   a.

   b.

3. If you ask me, Burger King has the best hamburgers in the world.

   a.

   b.

4. I believe all Americans love to watch baseball.

   a.

   b.

5. I think winter is the best season of the year.

   a.

   b.

V. Cultural Values

A. People from different cultures have different values. There are several of these values that we can use to generally describe Americans and people from your culture. Look at the values in the following list and try to match them to their characteristics.

1. Individualistic ____
2. Cooperative ____
3. Direct ____
4. Informal ____
5. Equal ____
6. Traditional ____
7. Competitive ____
8. Materialistic ____
9. Practical / Efficient ____
10. Private ____
11. Progressive ____
12. Formal ____

a. not hidden; easily understood

b. having a great interest in possessions, money, etc.

c. same in value, rank, etc.

d. working together

e. based on past principles, beliefs, etc.

f. casual; not formal

g. independent in thought or actions

h. having strong desire to be the best and succeed, usually on an individual basis

i. moving forward or developing continuously

j. not casual

k. personal; not to be shared with others

l. effective; convenient; working well without waste

B. Following are some situations that demonstrate some of the values listed on page 17. Match each situation or belief with a corresponding value.

Situation	*Corresponding Value(s)*
1. A student in your history class does not let you borrow her notes from the lecture because she is afraid that you might do better than she does on the next exam.	
2. Your next-door neighbor often spends money on new stereo and video equipment. He also usually buys a new car every three or four years.	
3. You just heard one of your classmates call your professor by her first name.	
4. One day after history class a student asks if you would like to join a study group to prepare for tomorrow's exam.	
5. People donate thousands of dollars to an organization that will be sending scientists to live on the planet Mars in the year 2020.	
6. A manager of a small company prefers that her employees call and refer to her as "Ms. Mead."	
7. A recent high school graduate will attend college this fall. She has saved money from working part-time during high school and plans to continue working part-time during college.	

C. Look at the following expressions and slogans (short advertising phrases) common in the United States. Which values do you think each one reflects?

    a. competition
    b. individualism
    c. materialism
    d. directness
    e. progress

1. _____ "I DID IT MY WAY."

2. _____ "It's the future that counts."

3. _____ **"HISTORY DOESN'T MATTER."**

4. _____ "Tell it like it is."

5. _____ "Look out for number one."

6. _____ **"Do your own thing."**

7. _____ "Have it your own way."

8. _____ "**Bigger** is better."

D. There are some obvious reasons for expecting people from a similar culture to act and think similarly, but there are other less obvious factors that are also important to consider. Look at the following chart. Scan the reading on pages 21–22 and fill in the chart with the appropriate information about the United States. Then, based on your own knowledge, fill in as much of the chart as possible about your country. Ignore the values column for now.

Factors Affecting Culture	Your Country	United States	Value(s)
Geographical location			
Size			
Foundation of the government			
When country was founded			
Religious background			

Scanning

A reading skill called scanning is used when you are looking for specific information in a reading passage. You do not read every word in the text; in fact, it is not important to understand every word in the text. All you want to do is find the necessary information. For example, think about when you read a newspaper in your native language. You might find an interesting article, but you probably do not read every word. Instead, you usually look for information such as when, how, or why something happened. Scanning is therefore done at a very high speed.

E. Carefully read the article "The Formation of Values in a Society."

THE FORMATION OF VALUES IN A SOCIETY

People from the same culture share several similar values. People evaluate objects, events, and behavior based on their values. How are these values formed? Let's look at some geographical, historical, and religious factors that have affected the value system in the United States.

Some factors that are important to the basis of values concern the geography of the country. The United States is the fourth largest nation in the world, covering 3,536,278 square miles (9,159,123 square kilometers). The amount of natural resources, including the land, fresh water, and animals, is abundant. The United States *comprises*, or makes up, a very large part of the North American continent. It is bordered by two large oceans and only two other countries, Mexico and Canada. If you drove the 2,825 miles (4,546 kilometers) from New York City to Los Angeles, it would take you at least 4–5 days, even if you only stopped to sleep, eat, and fill up your gas tank.

Second, several historical factors play an important role in the American value system. The United States was founded by a revolution; the early settlers of the United States opposed the *tyranny*, which is control with complete power, of many European rulers. The government was thus founded by settlers who had escaped controlling kings, churches, priests, and aristocrats. The new citizens of the United States put the power in the hands of the people by electing representatives to establish the laws and the foreign policy. This democracy is the oldest in the world, even though the country did not become established until 1776.

Last, at that time in Europe, there were major religious conflicts between Catholics and Protestants. Many people escaped from some of these European countries to the North American continent in order to have religious freedom. In fact, persecution—causing one to suffer for religious or political beliefs—was a major reason why many Protestants left different parts of Europe in the 17th century. Today, the existence of many Protestant *denominations*, such as Presbyterian, Baptist, Methodist, Lutheran, Episcopalian, reveal the religious diversity that developed in the United States. No one single church *dominates*, or controls, because the emphasis is on the individual and not one particular religion; the development of the United States was very much influenced by this emphasis on the individual.

Because of the diversity of the United States, it is impossible to claim that all Americans hold the same values. However, the large size of the country may cause many people to value their privacy and space. In addition, the historical and religious factors may help explain why many Americans are considered to be individualistic. Nevertheless, the development of any country is always in a state of *flux* (change), and although there are many factors that contribute to shaping cultural values, the geographical, historical, and religious factors are important to the change and growth of a country.

F. In order to understand the passage better, you need to know the meaning of many new words. Look at the following sentence. Based on the information in the sentence, can you write a definition of the italicized word? What clues did you use to do this?

"*Religious pluralism*—the coexistence of numerous distinct beliefs—is supported in the First Amendment of the United States Constitution."

Definition:

Language Clue(s):

Finding Definitions in a Text

Many times when you read something, the writer will provide a definition for certain vocabulary by using clues or phrases. Look at the following examples:

  a. *Values*, which are shared ideas or standards, are usually similar among people in the same culture.

In this example, the word "values" is defined by using the simple present tense of the verb *be*.

  An author will often use certain punctuation to help define words within a sentence. Look at the following two examples:

  b. The *pope* (leader of the Roman Catholic Church) acts as the bishop of Rome.
  c. *Persecution*—causing one to suffer for religious or political beliefs— was a major reason why many Protestants left different parts of Europe in the 17th century.

In the two sentences above, parentheses and dashes are used to help define words that an author believes need to be defined.

  Sometimes, the word is not clearly defined, but the writer provides an example that helps you make an intelligent guess about the meaning.

  d. Different *climates* in the United States, **such as** tropical, temperate, dry, and cold, also contribute to the diversity of lifestyles of Americans.

In this sentence the writer has given the examples of several different weather conditions to represent the word climates. The language clue, *such as*, is boldfaced.

G. Find the following words, which are italicized in the reading on pages 21–22. Write the language clue and then the definition of the word.

1. comprises

   language clue _____

   definition _____

2. tyranny

   language clue _____

   definition _____

3. denominations

   language clue _____

   definition _____

4. dominates

   language clue _____

   definition _____

5. flux

   language clue _____

   definition _____

H. Look back to the chart on page 20. Look at each of the factors again and based on what you learned in the reading, fill in the appropriate value(s).

Chapter 2

Speaking Out: How Americans Communicate

A. Look at the pictures of Americans talking. Also, think about other Americans that you have recently observed in person or on television and consider the following questions.

1. What do you observe about Americans and the way that they talk to one another? How is it different from your own culture?
2. What do you think is the pattern of American conversations? Does one person usually dominate or do people take turns?

A Look Behind/A Look Ahead

Culture influences the way that people communicate with one another. Misunderstandings can occur between people of different cultures simply due to different conversational patterns, subjects, and styles. In chapter 1, we talked about how people often stereotype or judge others. The foundation of basic American values was also outlined. In this chapter we will talk about the American style of communication so that you can avoid both making wrong judgments about Americans and avoid being wrongly judged by Americans. In addition, you will be able to see how values are also reflected in the way Americans communicate.

This chapter looks at certain communication functions, both verbal and nonverbal. Greetings (both formal and informal) and maintaining conversation with small talk as well as gestures and body language are considered important in learning to communicate in another language. The American style of these conversational tools may be very different from your own culture's style.

To the Student

After completing this chapter, you will be able to

1. recognize different types of introductions;
2. use titles in conversation where necessary;
3. initiate and maintain conversation—"small talk";
4. differentiate between acceptable/unacceptable small talk topics;
5. understand the meaning of several American gestures and other nonverbal clues.

Vocabulary Development

When words in English have more than one syllable, the word is pronounced with stress on one of the syllables. In the following word, there are three syllables, and the stress is on the first syllable.

ín tro vert

Listen to your teacher pronounce the words in the vocabulary list for this chapter and make an accent mark (´) above the syllable that has the stress. Then, go through the list and put a check (√) next to the words you know. When you are finished with the chapter, return to this list and make sure you can put a check next to all of the words. There is also room to list any additional words you have learned.

gesture	____	eye contact	____
nonverbal communication	____	compliment	____
address	____	greetings	____
interaction	____	encounter	____
small talk	____	introduction	____
proxemics	____	facial expression	____
farewell	____	universal	____
body language	____	introvert	____

reveal	____	gab	____
consultant	____	integrity	____
extrovert	____	cluster	____
pupil	____	pick up	____
close the sale	____		

Other:

_____   _____

_____   _____

_____   _____

_____   _____

I. Introductions and Other Encounters

A. Look at the table that follows. Imagine that you have to address the people. What titles would you use?

Person / Situation	Address
1. high school teacher named David Johnson	Mr. Johnson
2. child named Johnny Adams	Johnny
3. mayor named Jim Belzak	
4. your friend's mother named Karen Allen	
5. professor named Natalie Lefkowitz	
6. friend named Robert O'Neal	
7. senator named John Brinker	

B. After you meet someone, it is often necessary for you to introduce that person to a third party. Rank the expressions that Americans use to do this from the most formal (1) to the most informal (4).

Introduction	*Response*
____ Mitch, Susan, . . . Susan, Mitch.	Hi.
____ I'd like to introduce Dr. Jim Michaels.	How do you do?
____ This is Tom Byrd.	Nice to meet you.
____ I'd like you to meet Nelson.	It's a pleasure to meet you.

The ways that people use their bodies to greet one another may also differ, depending on the formality of the situation. In fact, these may also vary within one culture. A firm handshake and direct eye contact are common first-time greetings in the United States because they reflect honesty and directness.

As relationships between people progress, greetings between friends of the same sex and of different sex can vary. The American style of greetings between friends may be very different from your culture. In addition, it is important to consider the ethnic diversity of the United States and realize that many nationalities have brought their customs here and continue to practice them.

C. Look at the chart that follows and think about how people in the various relationships would use their bodies when they are speaking to each other. Compare the amount of space (proxemics), the type of greeting (verbal / physical), and the eye contact that are used between Americans and between people in your country.

Relationship	*Proxemics*	*Greeting*	*Eye Contact*

You—Employer
    United States
 	
    Your country			

Relationship	Proxemics	Greeting	Eye Contact
You—President or other government leader United States Your country			
You—Best friend United States Your country			

D. Farewells also differ in their degree of formality. Write the expressions of farewell that you hear. Rank each expression according to its level of formality (1 = least formal → 4 = most formal).

        Farewell Expression   *Formality*

1. _____   _____

2. _____   _____

3. _____   _____

4. _____   _____

E. Following are some situations in which you might greet someone or say good-bye to someone. What would you say in English in each case?

1. Saying goodnight to a child.

2. Saying good-bye after a job interview.

3. Going to a professor's office for help with a problem.

4. Saying good-bye to your teacher at the end of class.

5. Saying hello to a good friend.

II. American Conversation

A. Listen to a dialogue between Jan and Greg and answer these questions.

1. What kind of relationship do Jan and Greg have?
   a. brother-sister
   b. boyfriend-girlfriend
   c. new acquaintances
2. What is the topic of the conversation?
   a. sports
   b. work
   c. hometowns
3. Does either Jan or Greg dominate the conversation?

4. What do Jan and Greg have in common?

5. Jan and Greg are involved in a "small talk" conversation. What do you think small talk means? Why do you think Americans use "small" to describe this kind of conversation?

B. In groups of three or four, make lists of what you think are acceptable and unacceptable topics for initial small talk between Americans.

Acceptable Topics	Unacceptable Topics

C. Scan the following passage about small talk. Look for additional acceptable and unacceptable topics for small talk and add them to your list.

AMERICAN SMALL TALK

When Americans meet one another for the first time, they begin their conversation with "small talk." The topics of these conversations are very general and often situational—people start talking about anything in their common physical environment, such as the weather, the room in which they are standing or sitting, the food that they are eating, etc. Small talk is important because Americans are not very comfortable with silence. It is important, however, to know which topics are acceptable ("safe") and which are unacceptable ("unsafe") in American culture. Until Americans get to know one another better, certain acceptable small talk topics are usually the focus of conversations.

Situational topics like the weather are acceptable in many cultures, but they obviously cannot be discussed for a long period of time. Asking someone about his/her occupation is also very common, especially for Americans, who place a high value on working. Questions of taste could also be asked. For example, one could ask a person if she has heard the latest CD by Michael Jackson or Elton John, which may lead to a deeper discussion about musical preferences. Compliments are common conversation starters. Last, in a country like the United States where people move so often, places of origin are often discussed and nonnative students will probably be asked by Americans about their country and their impressions of the United States.

There are many topics, however, that are inappropriate to use in starting conversation. For example, religion is considered a very personal matter. One could ask about general religious practices in the United States, but in general people must not ask others directly about their personal religious practices during small talk. Politics is usually another unacceptable topic. Americans tend to avoid the subject, especially if it is obvious that all parties do not have the same beliefs. Two other subjects will immediately make Americans uncomfortable: age and money. Americans value youth, so many Americans want to keep their age a secret. Regarding financial matters, income and the price of possessions are also personal matters and should not be used to start a conversation with an American. For example, if you compliment someone on her sweater or shoes, asking the cost of the items is inappropriate.

Being aware of these acceptable and unacceptable topics may help people from other cultures feel more comfortable around Americans they are meeting for the first time. Listening to American small talk has often led nonnatives to make wrong judgments about an American's ability to carry on a conversation. Culture, however, influences the way that people communicate with one another. Learning about this feature of conversation will help you understand Americans better.

D. Write three questions about appropriate topics that you might ask someone you have met for the first time.

Example:

(weather)   What do you think about this hot weather?

1.

2.

3.

E. Listen to each of the following dialogues and write the topic(s) of each conversation. Then decide whether the entire small talk conversation is acceptable (safe) or unacceptable (unsafe).

1. Topic _____ A or U

2. Topic _____ A or U

3. Topic _____ A or U

4. Topic _____ A or U

F. When giving someone advice, *must*, *should*, and *could* are often used. Look back at the reading on "American Small Talk" and underline the sentences containing these words. What is the difference between *must*, *should*, and *could*?

Modals of Advice and Suggestion

These modals are followed by the simple form of the verb.

Example:

"He *doesn't ask* their ages."   →   "He *should never* ask their ages."

Should	Something is advised, but you make the choice.
	"You *should try* to meet more people."
Should not	It is advised that you *not* do something. The contraction is *shouldn't.*
	"He *should not call* her by her first name."
Must not	Something is prohibited. It is very important that you *not* do something. The contraction is *mustn't.*
	"You *mustn't be* too afraid to meet people."
Could	Something is suggested as a possible future action.
	"She *could ask* him to dinner on Friday."

G. Reread the passage "American Small Talk." On a separate sheet of paper, write a letter to a friend at home explaining how to make small talk with Americans. Remember to mention the acceptable and unacceptable topics. Use the phrases below to help you.

"You could (ask/inquire about/talk about) . . ."
"You should . . ."
"You should not (ask/inquire about/talk about) . . ."
"You must not. . ."

H. Maintaining a balance in a conversation with Americans is also important. Americans become uncomfortable if people ask too many questions, and they also become frustrated if their own questions are repeatedly answered with only one- or two-word responses. Listen to the following dialogue between two students. Think about the following questions as you listen.

1. What is the topic of the conversation? Is it acceptable or unacceptable?

2. Why does John decide to stop talking to Amy?

3. What should Amy have done to make the conversation more successful?

I. Look at the conversation from the previous activity that you heard between John and Amy. With your partner, use your suggestions and change the dialogue so that it is a successful example of American small talk.

John:	Hi! You're in English 406 with Dr. McGorman, aren't you?
Amy:	Yeah, <u>but that class is really a lot of work. Is this your first course with McGorman?</u>
John:	<u>No, it's my second. It's a difficult course, but she's a great professor.</u> Do you like that novel we're reading now?
Amy:	Not really. _____.
	_____?
John:	_____.
	Are you an English major?
Amy:	Yes. _____.
	_____?
John:	_____.
	How long have you been at Morton College?
Amy:	Two years. _____.
	_____?

III. Nonverbal Communication

A. Read the following quotation and answer the questions.

A person cannot *not* communicate. Though she may decide to stop talking, it is impossible for her to stop behaving. The behavior of a person—her facial expressions, posture, gestures, and other actions—provides an uninterrupted stream of information and a constant source of clues to the feelings she is experiencing. The reading of body language, therefore, is one of the most significant skills of good listening. (Robert Bolton, *People Skills* [New York: Simon & Schuster, 1979], 78)

1. What do you think "a person cannot *not* communicate" means?

2. What types of behavior make up nonverbal communication?

3. Why should you pay attention to someone's body language?

B. Human beings often use their hands and faces to express meaning. These movements are called gestures. Gestures are not universal; certain gestures have the exact opposite meaning in different cultures. The body language of cultures is therefore a very important one to learn. Several of the most "well-meaning" American gestures can often offend those from other countries.
   Match each gesture with its appropriate meaning.

1. ____ "I don't know."   5. ____ "Stop. That's enough."

2. ____ "That's great!"   6. ____ "Oh no! I forgot."

3. ____ "I didn't hear you."   7. ____ "Good luck."

4. ____ "Come here."   8. ____ "OK."

a.

b.

c.

d.

e.

f.

g.

h.

C. There are also many idioms in English that use parts of the body to express an idea. What do you think "keep your chin up" means? Can you think of some idioms or proverbs in your language that use parts of the body to express meaning?

D.

1. Work with a partner and try to match the following idioms with their meanings.

   a. tongue-tied   f. by heart
   b. to bend over backwards   g. to pay through the nose
   c. at your fingertips   h. elbow grease
   d. to put our heads together   i. to have a sweet tooth
   e. see eye to eye   j. to shake a leg

   1. ___ to crave something with sugar

   2. ___ to agree

   3. ___ to spend too much money for something

   4. ___ to try really hard to do something

   5. ___ to work (physically) hard on something

   6. ___ to hurry

   7. ___ to be very available

   8. ___ to work together on a problem or project

   9. ___ not able to talk

   10. ___ to memorize

2. Use the expressions that you have learned in the sentences that follow.

   1. My son's English teacher does everything she can for her students. She _____ to make sure that the students understand everything.

   2. I had to learn all the new vocabulary words _____.

   3. Ginny told Deana to _____ or else they would be late for her dentist appointment.

   4. "If we _____," Amy said, "we will be able to finish the plan for the new park by tomorrow."

   5. When the teacher asked Andy why he hadn't finished his home work, he became _____.

   6. "Everything you need is _____," was the slogan for the hotel we stayed at last summer.

E. Look at the title of the newspaper article on page 40. Based on this title and what you have learned about so far in this chapter, what do you predict this reading will be about? Write down any words or phrases in the following space that represent what the text will be about.

Predicting and Previewing

You have just used one reading skill: predicting. Another reading skill is previewing. Both of these skills give you enough information about the text so that you begin to think about it and form opinions about it. Then when you read the text, you understand it better. Predicting and previewing help you to read more effectively.

ACTIONS
SPEAK LOUDER THAN
WORDS

Body language can give away hidden feelings

By CARLA WHEELER
and CARLA A. CLARKSON
Gannett News Service

Bodies gab.

And they usually speak louder than words.

The way people cross their ankles, shake your hand, smile and fold their arms says a lot about them, says Phil Miller, a consultant in Fullerton, Calif., who conducts workshops on body language.

"The body does what the mind is thinking," says Miller, who started to study body signals more than 40 years ago while serving in the Marines. "Your body always says something. People who read body language can pick up what your true feelings are."

Knowing the meaning behind someone's body moves and learning how to put your best body language forward can help you personally and professionally, according to Miller, who also works with politicians as an image consultant.

For example, if you're a salesperson and a client you've just met allows you into what they consider their personal space, it might be OK to try to close the sale, Miller says. A person's personal space is usually 3$^1/_2$ feet to the front, 18 inches to the back and six inches to each side, he says.

"If someone will allow you in their space, they're beginning to trust you," Miller says.

Another way to find out if someone likes or trusts you is to look at the pupils of their eyes, Miller says. If a person is interested in you or what you're saying, the pupils of their eyes will get bigger, he says. "If the pupils get smaller, it's the opposite—they don't like

---

WHAT IT MEANS

- **Pursing the lips:** Disapproval or concentration.
- **Licking the lips:** Nervousness.
- **Biting the lip:** Self-reproach.
- **Tapping the foot:** Nervousness, impatience or annoyance.
- **Tilting the head to one side:** Sympathy; she's listening closely.
- **Looking at you sideways:** Mistrust.
- **Putting the hands behind the back:** Uncomfortable or defensive, afraid of what she might reveal.

---

you or what you're talking about," Miller says. There are two basic body positions—open and closed—which are key indicators of a person's feelings, says Dr. Judith Graser, clinical psychologist in Washington, D.C.

"Often people are revealing a position and they aren't even aware of it."

A person in a closed position usually will lean away, cross their arms and legs and try to distance themselves from the person they are talking to, Graser said.

When a person is talking with their body in an open position, they are leaning forward and are relaxed.

Experts agree that a person should never be judged by one sign alone, such as interpreting legs or arms that are crossed.

Terry Williams of the Terry Williams Agency, a public relations firm in New York, says body language is important when interacting with another person or a business.

"If you are confident and truthful, you will be open and direct as far as your body language is concerned," she says. "When there are a cluster of closed positions used, there may be a question about the person's confidence and integrity."

From Gannett News Service in the *Lansing State Journal*, July 22, 1993, "Today" section.

F. Preview the text by reading it as quickly as possible. You can do this by reading the title, the subheadings, and the first sentence of every paragraph. Write down all the vocabulary and the ideas that you remember.

G. Carefully reread the article "Actions Speak Louder than Words" that appeared in the *Lansing State Journal.*

H. Answer the following questions based on the article.

1. According to Miller, how can knowing the meaning behind someone's body moves and learning how to put your best body language forward help you?

2. What is a person's desirable personal space?

3. What does it mean if someone allows you into their personal space?

4. What are the two basic body positions?

I. Match the following words from the reading with their definitions.

gab   consultant   cluster   pick up
integrity   close the sale   pupil   reveal

1. _____   a person who gives professional advice to others

2. _____   to talk continuously (informal)

3. _____ a number of things of the same kind together

4. _____ to notice

5. _____ to settle; to complete something

6. _____ the small black round opening in the middle of the eye

7. _____ honesty; trustworthiness

8. _____ to show; to make known

J. Fill in the missing verbs of the sentences from the article.

1. "If you're a salesperson and a client you've just met allows you into what they consider their personal space, it _____ OK to try to close the sale."

2. "If a person is interested in what you're saying, the pupils of their eyes _____ bigger."

3. "If you are confident and truthful, you _____ open and direct as far as your body language is concerned."

Conditionals: Future Predictive Conditions

"If" clauses often express a time in the future, but they can use the present tense. The following sentence expresses a condition that predicts a future situation, not necessarily a general fact or habit.

If a person *crosses* her ankles, she *may be* afraid.

Notice that the result clause ("she *may be* afraid") uses a modal with a simple verb. Remember, *will* shows that the result is certain if the condition is met, and *may, might,* and *could* show that the result is possible.

K. Look at the box "What It Means" in the newspaper article. Write sentences using future predictive conditionals based on the nonverbal clues and emotions given. You may need to change nouns into verbs or adjectives.

Example:

   If a person purses her lips, she might disapprove of something.

   1.

   2.

   3.

   4.

   5.

   6.

L. Answer the following questions.

   1. Do you think you are a private, shy, quiet (introverted) person? Do you think you are an outgoing and talkative (extroverted) person?

   2. Do you think more in words and numbers or do you think more in words and pictures?

   3. Which types of careers are you more drawn to: (1) research, law, accounting, engineering, and politics, (2) or art, music, writing, acting, and nursing?

M. Cross your arms in front of your chest and look at the diagram that follows. Does the way you cross your arms give clues to your personality?

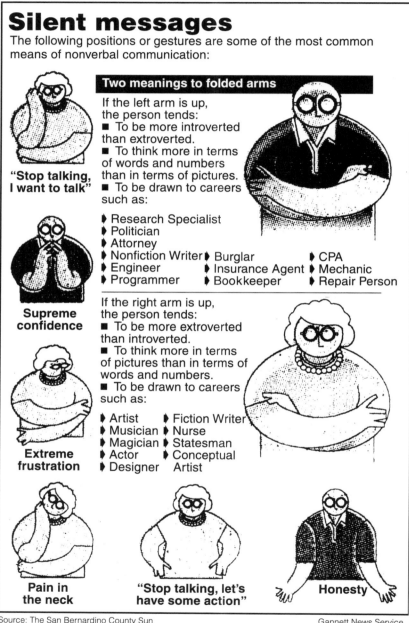

Silent messages

The following positions or gestures are some of the most common means of nonverbal communication:

"Stop talking, I want to talk"

Supreme confidence

Extreme frustration

Pain in the neck

Two meanings to folded arms

If the left arm is up, the person tends:
- To be more introverted than extroverted.
- To think more in terms of words and numbers than in terms of pictures.
- To be drawn to careers such as:

- Research Specialist
- Politician
- Attorney
- Nonfiction Writer
- Engineer
- Programmer

- Burglar
- Insurance Agent
- Bookkeeper

- CPA
- Mechanic
- Repair Person

If the right arm is up, the person tends:
- To be more extroverted than introverted.
- To think more in terms of pictures than in terms of words and numbers.
- To be drawn to careers such as:

- Artist
- Musician
- Magician
- Actor
- Designer

- Fiction Writer
- Nurse
- Statesman
- Conceptual Artist

"Stop talking, let's have some action"

Honesty

Source: The San Bernardino County Sun

Gannett News Service

Redrawn from Gannett News Service in the *Lansing State Journal*, July 22, 1993, "Today" section.

IV. Values Application

A. Look at the different statements that describe American conversation and decide which American value(s) each one represents. Choose among the values that we talked about on page 17. An example has been done for you.

Statements	*Value*
1. Salary is an unsafe topic in American small talk.	Privacy
2. Conversation between two people is like a Ping-Pong game.	_____
3. Even though you should not call your professors by their first names immediately, some of them prefer this.	_____
4. Americans usually stand about 3.5 feet away from each other.	_____
5. Americans may think you are not paying attention if you do not look directly into their eyes.	_____

Chapter 3

Shopping Around: Consumerism in the United States

Make a guess at the best answer for the following questions concerning American supermarkets. Do these numbers surprise you?

1. How many different hair shampoos are available in a typical American supermarket?
   a. About 20
   b. Over 35
2. How long are the supermarket shelves that contain laundry detergent?
   a. About 30 feet (9.1 meters) long
   b. About 60 feet (18.3 meters) long
3. How many types of breakfast cereal can one generally find?
   a. About 100
   b. About 50
4. How many different kinds of *one* popular brand of dog food are available?
   a. About 5
   b. About 10
5. How many different kinds of hand soap do you think are available?
   a. About 20
   b. About 50

Calvin and Hobbes   by Bill Watterson

What is funny about the comic strip? How is it related to American values?

A Look Behind/A Look Ahead

In chapter 2, you briefly learned about one aspect of little-c culture—the way that Americans communicate with one another. In this chapter and the ones that follow, you will continue to study little-c culture—the lifestyle of Americans. American consumerism, which includes where and how Americans spend and save money, for example, may be very different from your own culture.

To the Student

After completing this chapter, you will be able to

1. identify different types of shops in the United States;
2. examine the history of supermarkets;
3. recognize various ways that Americans save money on their purchases;
4. understand the use of credit cards;
5. apply the different values that are present in American consumerism.

Vocabulary Development

Vocabulary Guessing Strategies: Word Morphology

When you read something in English, there may be some words that you do not understand. Because it takes time to look up these words in the dictionary, it will help you to learn some strategies for guessing the meaning of these words. One way to do this is to look at the *morphology* of the word, or parts of the word.

A word can consist of a prefix, a base, and a suffix. Not every word, however, will have a prefix and/or a suffix. A *prefix* is one or more syllables that can be added to the front of a word or base, while a *suffix* can be added to the end. Their function is to change the meaning of the word. Many prefixes and suffixes come from Latin or Greek.

Look at the following word that you used in chapter 1:

COOPERATION
prefix   base   suffix

The meanings of the prefix, base, and suffix are as follows:

Co = with, together
operat(e) = to work, to be in action (verb base)
tion = noun suffix

Therefore, we can guess that the word "cooperation" is a noun that means the act of working together.

A. The following charts lists some common prefixes, their meanings, and an example of a word with that prefix. There are blank spaces in the example column. Fill in these blanks with a word that you have learned in this text.

Prefix	Meaning	Example
a-	without, not	atypical
ante-	before	antecedent
anti-	against	antifreeze
auto-	self	autonomous

con-, com-, col-, co-	together, with	_____
de-	reverse, opposite	devalue
ethn-	race or people	_____
e-, ex-	out from	_____
inter-	between, among	_____
mis-	wrong	misunderstand
pre-	before	_____
re-	back, again	_____
self-	independent, by oneself	self-help
un-	not	_____

B. Underline the suffixes in the following words. An example has been done for you.

superfic<u>ial</u>	anthropologist	inferior	awareness	cultural
favorably	generalize	institution	conceivable	integrate
acquaintance	distinctive	collectively	ethnocentrism	ideology

Now, place the suffixes that indicate if a word is a noun, verb, adjective, or adverb into their appropriate place in the chart.

Noun Suffixes	*Verb Suffixes*
Adjective Suffixes -ial	*Adverb Suffixes*

C. Finally, many of the base, or root, words have specific meanings that may help you understand the meanings of new words.

Base	Meaning
duc	lead
flect	bend
sequ	follow
anthro	human
man	hand
morph	form, structure
onym	name

Using your charts on prefixes, suffixes, and bases, make a list of some words that you have learned so far in this textbook and write their definitions.

1.

2.

3.

4.

5.

6.

7.

8.

D. Look at the following vocabulary words from this chapter. Next to the word, write an N if you think the word is a noun, V if the word is a verb, A if the word is an adjective, and AV if the word is an adverb. Use any suffixes in the words to help you. Next, see if there are any prefixes or root words that can help you guess the meaning of the word. When you are finished with the chapter, return to this list to make sure you understand all of the words.

credit limit	____	specialty	____
purchase	____	brand name	____
consumer	____	debt	____
payment	____	convenience	____
thrifty	____	secondhand	____
florist	____	appliance	____
bakery	____	transaction	____
supermarket	____	self-service	____
household	____	coupon	____
hardware	____	charge	____
finance	____		

I. Where Americans Shop: Types of Stores

A. Where do Americans shop for the goods and services that they are interested in buying? Look at the following pictures of different types of places where you can buy things in the United States. Match the pictures to their appropriate name from the list provided.

1. ____ hardware store

2. ____ drugstore

3. ____ department store

4. ____ bakery

5. ____ appliance store

6. ____ florist

7. ____ sporting goods store

a.

b.

c.

d.

e.

f.

g.

B. In the column on the right is a list of some items that would be available in the stores that you looked at in the previous activity. Write the name of the type of store where these items can be found.

Type of Store	General Items Available
	medicine, candy, magazines, shampoo
	refrigerators, washing machines, stereos, stoves, dryers, dishwashers
	paint, hammers, screwdrivers, nails, wallpaper, shovels, garden supplies
	clothing, jewelry, linen, perfume, sunglasses, hats, socks
	skis, tennis rackets, bats, Frisbees, fishing poles

C. Even though different specialty shops are available in the United States, you will probably not find very many Americans who go to a bakery to buy bread or a drugstore to buy shampoo. Going to supermarkets, which are found all over the United States and in many other countries, is a much more popular way to shop. Shampoo, bread, meat, fresh flowers, and even some hardware supplies are available at supermarkets. You are going to hear a lecture about supermarkets in the United States. Before you hear the lecture, briefly discuss the following questions:

1. Why do you think that most Americans prefer shopping at supermarkets to shopping at different specialty shops?

2. Are large supermarkets popular in your country? Why or why not?

D. Listen to the first part of the lecture and answer the questions that follow.

1. This lecture will be about which of the following?
   a. the comparison between various supermarkets around the world
   b. the history of supermarkets
   c. the structure of supermarkets
2. What words did the speaker say that helped you answer this question?

Lecture Organization

There are many language clues you can listen for that will help you understand the organization of a talk. Understanding the organization will help you make predictions about what the person will say, and will also help you to remember information better because it is related to something.

Introductory Clues

Some lecturers state their goals very clearly such as "Today I will talk about X," or "I'd like to cover three goals." Other speakers may not state their purpose very clearly. As a listener, you generally should not worry about taking notes during the introduction. Instead, listen carefully to see if you can understand the purpose and organization of the entire talk.

Chronological Clues

In the lecture on the history of the supermarket, several language clues are used to organize the lecture. These clues are important to help the listener follow the history of supermarkets in the United States. The dominant organizational pattern the authors use is chronology, which provides the reader with a time frame. Some language clues a writer can use with this organizational pattern include *first, next, in 1988, two years later,* and *soon.*

Can you think of any other possible time clues?

E. Read the following two sentences. Underline the expressions that indicate *when* these events took place.

   1. Prewrapped meat was introduced in the 1950s to save shoppers time.
   2. Sylvan Goldman first introduced the shopping cart in Oklahoma in 1936. Later, he invented luggage carts that are used in airports.

F. Listen to the lecture for the main ideas. In addition, listen for any language clues of time and write them in the blank spaces in the lecture outline. Do not attempt to take any notes at this time.

LECTURE ON THE HISTORY OF SUPERMARKETS

Supermarkets = stores that sell most household items

   Self-serve =

Early 1800s—general stores with food items

   _____

   Specialty stores were introduced
         e.g.,

20th century

   _____

1930

_____   1,200 self-service supermarkets

During WWII

Recently

G. Now listen to the lecture and take notes using the guide provided. Listen for the various time clues that are used and write the main ideas of the lectures.

II. Thrifty Shopping

A. You now know *where* Americans shop, but the way that Americans spend their money may be different from the spending habits of people in your culture. How can you save money when you shop? American stores often offer sales during special times of the year, but there are other ways to save money. Get into groups and brainstorm different ways that you can save money when you shop for food, clothing, household goods, etc.

_____

_____

_____

Are you a thrifty shopper? Which person in your group do you think is the thriftiest shopper? Do you think it is worth the extra time and effort to save a little extra money?

B. Americans often try to get rid of used items by having a sale outside their house, in the yard or garage. These types of sales are an American invention referred to as "garage" sales or "yard" sales. Look at the following classified ads about garage sales from the local newspaper. Answer the questions that follow.

718 Garage/Estate Sales Hill Valley

Beech St., 463 Moving / Garage Sale. Furniture, student books, 4 bikes, children's clothing, microwave, and lots of household necessities. Fri. & Sat. Aug 14-15, 8-5.

Carlito Ct., 272 10 year sale. Lots of stuff & everything must go. Students, renters, and homeowners are welcome!! There is something for everyone!! Friday, 8/14 from 9-3.

Walnut Dr., 6262 Four family garage sale. Rain or shine because everything must go! New and second-hand designer clothing for men, women, & children. Furniture, toys, radios, televisions, stereo equipment, pet supplies, antiques, sporting goods. Sat., Aug 15, 8-3.

Sheller Ln., 7637 Sat. 8-4. Dinette set, twin bed & box spring, toys, video games, luggage, pet supplies, lamps, some antiques and much more!!

Thomas Ave., 7432 Estate of Dr. William Patterson. Sun., Aug 16, 8-4. Living room, dining, bdrm. & kitchen; refrigerator, dresser, dishes, and glasses; dinette w/4 chairs; rocker, wood stove, trunk, small collectibles. Storage cabinets, various lawn tools; power tools; antique desks. Cash or check with proper I.D.

Zimmer Dr., 867 Huge Garage Sale. Moving out of country! All items must be sold! Bedroom, dining, kitchen, family, and living room furniture. Fri. & Sat. Aug 14-15, 9-6.

1. At which two addresses are pet supplies available?

2. At which address will the 10 year sale take place? What do you think a 10 year sale is?

3. Where can you find secondhand designer clothing? What does *secondhand* mean?

4. What time does the garage sale on Beech St. begin?

5. Does the garage sale on Carlito Ct. continue on Saturday?

6. What day is the estate sale of Dr. William Patterson? Who do you think is holding this estate sale? Why?

C. Art would like to have a garage sale next Friday, so he decided to call the local paper to arrange an advertisement. Listen to the conversation between Art and the associate in the classified ads department of the local newspaper. Write down the most important information regarding the sale and then write an advertisement that will appear in the paper.

Classified Advertisement Information

_____

_____

_____

Now get into groups and write one advertisement that will appear in next week's paper. Use the sample ads in Activity B on page 57 to guide you.

Garage/Estate Sales

_____

_____

_____

_____

_____

_____

D. Coupons are another way to save money. Look at the following coupon, which appeared in the *Kalamazoo Gazette*. Get into groups and answer the questions that follow.

1. What is the brand name of the product in the coupon?

2. How much money can a consumer save if he or she buys this brand of adhesive bandages?

3. Is it possible to use this coupon on the Sport Strip™ type of Band-Aids®?

4. Which company produces Band-Aid® adhesive bandages?

5. What does "limit one per purchase" mean?

6. Where can you usually find coupons?

E. You are grocery shopping at GLD Foods. Read your coupons and shopping list carefully and calculate how much money you will have to pay at the checkout counter without coupons and with coupons. (There is no tax on grocery items today!!)

Shopping List	
One box of Swiss Miss® Hot Cocoa	$2.70/ea.
One can of Eagle® Brand Sweetened Condensed Milk	$1.39/ea.
One 22 oz. bottle of Ivory® Dishwashing Liquid	$2.29/ea.
One bottle of Bold® Liquid Detergent	$3.99/ea.
One bottle of Head & Shoulders® Shampoo	$2.89/ea.
One 7 oz. can of SPAM® Luncheon Meat	$.99/ea.
One bottle of Johnson's *baby*® shampoo	$2.39/ea.

Total without coupons $ _____

Total with coupons $ _____

GLD Foods offers *double coupons* every Wednesday. This usually means that all valid coupons up to 50 cents are worth double their face value. How much would you pay for these groceries on a double coupon day?

Total with double coupons $ _____

III. How Americans Shop: Credit Cards

Visa and the flag design are registered trademarks of VISA International. Reprinted with permission.

A. In small groups, answer the questions that follow:

1. What are the names of some popular credit cards?

2. Do you have any credit cards? If yes, how many? If no, do you think that you will get a credit card one day? Why?

3. Can anyone get a credit card? What are some of the requirements for obtaining a credit card?

B. Look at the credit card bill that follows and answer the questions that follow.

New Castle Bank Credit Card Services   Closing Date: March 31, 19--

Summary of Account			
		previous balance	$235.80
		payments & credits	$196.98
card number	7588 7747 8837 0003	purchases	$360.78
		interest (finance charges)	$5.59
credit limit	$3,000.00		
credit available	$2,594.81	**present balance**	**$405.19**

To avoid additional interest charges, pay the entire present balance by . . .	*April 27, 19--*

All transactions of this period

payments & credits

2/25/95	payment – **THANK YOU**	−$100.00
2/28/95	credit – Van Heller's Department Store	−$96.98

purchases

3/4/95	Goodlittle's Pet Supplies	Ann Arbor, MI	$25.09
3/7/95	Scheller's Rent-A-Car	Lansing, MI	$89.98
3/7/95	Van Heller's Department Store	Orland Park, IL	$15.44
3/8/95	Jocundry's Books	E. Lansing, MI	$12.34
3/10/95	Fairview Hotel	Bloomington, IN	$69.63
3/18/95	Hub's Gas	Mt. Pleasant, MI	$23.87
3/26/95	Hidy's Mechanics	Lansing, MI	$124.43

1. How much was my payment on February 25 to the New Castle Bank Credit Card Services?

2. How many different times did I use my credit card between March 4 and March 31?

3. At which department store did I use my credit card in Illinois?

4. What were my finance charges (interest) for this past month?

5. How much credit is currently available on my credit card?

6. On what date should the bill be paid?

C. Which do you think is better to use—cash or credit cards? Get into groups and write down a list of advantages and disadvantages of using cash and using credit cards.

Using Cash	*Using Credit Cards*
Advantages	*Advantages*
Disadvantages	*Disadvantages*

D. For which of the following products or services would you use a credit card? Why or why not?

renting a car	a plane ticket	a Big Mac® at McDonald's
reserving a hotel room	a new car	a TV at a garage sale
a cup of coffee	a new house	a new TV at an appliance store

IV. Values Application

A. Read the following statements made by a group of Americans. Which of the values that we talked about do each of these statements reflect?

    a. Privacy
    b. Efficiency / Practicality
    c. Materialism
    d. Competition

1. _____ "I like to be able to walk into a large supermarket and be able to choose the items that I want on my own. I don't like anyone to bother me while I'm shopping."

2. _____ "Because of the large number of brand items that are available (e.g., toothpaste), different companies have to constantly improve the quality of their items as well as keep the prices down in order to keep up."

3. _____ "I usually save between ten to fifteen dollars on groceries every week with coupons."

4. _____ "I like to be able to park my car quickly, run into the supermarket, and buy everything I need within 15 minutes. I don't like to go to two or three different places to purchase my food."

5. _____ "I have several different credit cards and I have a lot of debts, but I enjoy being able to buy things for my house such as a new stereo, big screen TV, and personal computer."

6. _____ "Why should I buy a 21 inch television when I can get a 27 inch one?"

B. What is most important to you when you go shopping in your own country? Is choice important? Is convenience important? Do you like to interact with people when you shop or would you rather shop without talking to people?

Chapter 4

Hitting the Books: The American Education System

Find the names of the subjects listed that are taught in American schools (nursery school through university). You'll have to look horizontally (side to side), vertically (up and down), and diagonally.

```
B  S  G  R  E  H  R  D  H  W  E  N  G  L  I  S  H  T  H  O
O  I  M  A  T  H  F  A  R  B  E  G  L  A  D  G  H  B  E  D
B  E  O  W  L  O  G  H  K  R  N  S  N  N  I  N  G  N  A  P
S  L  F  L  W  B  R  A  Y  B  N  S  T  G  G  R  L  S  N  G
E  F  F  D  O  G  A  Y  H  A  O  Y  Y  U  E  A  F  O  O  F
D  B  B  Y  O  G  E  R  A  N  W  P  I  A  F  M  S  H  O  T
S  U  N  A  D  Q  Y  E  R  T  R  S  N  G  A  T  A  M  E  S
C  J  T  W  W  W  S  U  R  H  K  Y  W  E  D  E  S  N  E  U
I  H  U  O  O  G  S  E  T  R  I  S  Q  A  A  K  C  T  O  I
M  Q  I  O  R  K  C  E  I  O  N  I  J  R  G  N  I  P  Y  T
O  W  N  W  K  T  I  R  W  P  H  A  R  T  F  G  M  M  I  N
N  S  I  R  I  S  T  X  G  O  F  N  F  S  H  I  O  R  O  T
O  F  T  K  N  D  S  N  Z  L  A  T  C  R  P  E  N  O  R  Y
C  D  L  E  G  H  I  X  N  O  N  I  T  K  Y  T  O  R  O  G
E  A  E  C  A  T  T  W  E  G  S  W  K  G  R  H  C  K  S  T
O  F  F  O  E  S  A  E  H  Y  W  G  N  I  D  A  E  R  U  H
R  T  S  K  F  F  T  S  H  E  F  G  E  C  O  T  E  N  A  D
C  G  R  S  H  F  S  P  E  L  L  I  N  G  Q  G  M  A  R  T
I  A  A  Q  G  R  W  F  J  D  S  A  Y  X  J  S  O  M  O  M
M  N  O  I  T  A  C  U  D  E  L  A  C  I  S  Y  H  P  I  T
```

spelling	algebra	statistics	biology
marketing	reading	anthropology	language arts
microeconomics	woodworking	physics	English
physical education	home economics	typing	

After you are finished with the chapter, return to this page and decide at which level of American education each of the subjects is usually taught.

A Look Behind/A Look Ahead

In chapter 3, we looked at American consumerism—how and where Americans shop. In this chapter we'll explore the American education system. You will discover when and where Americans go to school and what they study. Because education is a complex issue, this chapter will only provide an overview of the American educational system. You will, however, be able to recognize the values that exist in the system.

To the Student

After completing this chapter, you will be able to

1. identify some aspects of the American philosophy of education;
2. understand the organization of the American school system;
3. analyze the changes in American school enrollment;
4. describe American higher education;
5. identify some important problems and issues in American public education.

After completing this chapter, return to this page and assess your own achievement in reaching these objectives.

Vocabulary Development

A good English-English dictionary can tell you much more about a word than just the meaning. Each dictionary will probably use slightly different abbreviations and formats; however, the following entry from *The Random House Unabridged Dictionary*, 2d ed. should be consistent with most dictionaries. The specifics about your dictionary will be explained in the front of the dictionary.

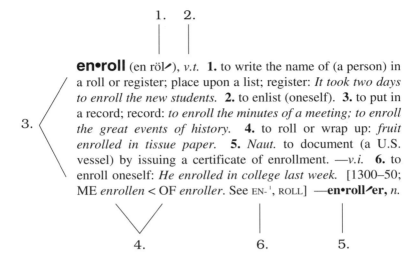

1. 2.

en•roll (en rōl⁀), *v.t.* **1.** to write the name of (a person) in a roll or register; place upon a list; register: *It took two days to enroll the new students.* **2.** to enlist (oneself). **3.** to put in a record; record: *to enroll the minutes of a meeting; to enroll the great events of history.* **4.** to roll or wrap up: *fruit enrolled in tissue paper.* **5.** *Naut.* to document (a U.S. vessel) by issuing a certificate of enrollment. —*v.i.* **6.** to enroll oneself: *He enrolled in college last week.* [1300–50; ME *enrollen* < OF *enroller.* See EN-¹, ROLL] —**en•roll⁀er,** *n.*

3.

4. 6. 5.

A. Put the number from the dictionary entry on the line next to its corresponding explanation.

_____ Etymology (history of the word)

_____ Part of speech (verb, noun, adjective, etc.)

_____ Meaning(s) of the word

_____ Cross references

_____ Inflected forms (how the form of the word changes, usually by changing the ending, to indicate different usages)

_____ Syllabification, pronunciation

B. Now look at the entire page of entries on page 71. Scan it quickly for answers to the following questions.

1. How many syllables does the word *enormous* have? What symbol does this dictionary use to separate the syllables?

Dictionary entry from *The Random House Unabridged Dictionary,* 2d ed. (New York: Random House, 1993).

2. Where is the stress in the word *enrapture?* What symbol is used to show where the stress is?

3. What different parts of speech is the word *enough?*

4. What are the undefined forms for the word *enslave?*

5. From what three languages did the word *ensign* come?

6. For certain words, many dictionaries also provide synonyms (different words that have a similar meaning). What are two synonyms for the word *enrage?*

noblir. See EN-[1], NOBLE] —**en·no′ble·ment,** *n.* —**en·no′bler,** *n.* —**en·no′bling·ly,** *adv.*

En·no·sig·ae·us (en′ə sig′ē əs), *n. Class. Myth.* an epithet of Poseidon, meaning "earth-shaker."

en·nui (än wē′, än′wē; *Fr.* äɴ nwē′), *n.* a feeling of utter weariness and discontent resulting from satiety or lack of interest; boredom: *The endless lecture produced an unbearable ennui.* [1660–70; < F: boredom; OF *enui* displeasure; see ANNOY]
—**Syn.** listlessness, tedium, lassitude, languor.

E·noch (ē′nək), *n.* **1.** the father of Methuselah. Gen. 5:22. **2.** a son of Cain. Gen. 4:17. **3.** a male given name: from a Hebrew word meaning "teacher."

E′noch Ar′den (är′dn), **1.** (*italics*) a narrative poem (1864) by Tennyson. **2.** its hero. **3.** a missing person who is presumed dead but is later found to be alive.

e·no·ki (e nok′ē), *n.* a thin, long-stemmed and tiny-capped white mushroom, *Flamma velutipes,* native to the northern mountain ranges of Japan and prized as a food. [< Japn *enoki(-take),* equiv. to *enoki* hackberry, Chinese nettle tree (< **ey no kiy;* **ai* hackberry + *no* particle + **koy* tree) + *take* mushroom]

e·nol (ē′nôl, ē′nol), *n. Chem.* an organic compound containing a hydroxyl group attached to a doubly linked carbon atom, as in >C=C(OH)−. [1935–40; appar. < Gk (*h*)*én* one (neut.) + -OL[1]] —**e·nol·ic** (ē nol′ik), *adj.*

E·no·la (i nō′lə), *n.* a female given name.

Eno′la Gay′, the name of the American B-29 bomber, piloted by Col. Paul Tibbets, Jr., that dropped the atomic bomb on Hiroshima, Japan, on Aug. 6, 1945.

e·no·late (ēn′l āt′), *n. Chem.* any metallic derivative of an enol. [1960–65; ENOL + -ATE[2]]

e·no·lize (ēn′l īz′), *v.t., v.i.,* **-lized, -liz·ing.** *Chem.* to convert into an enol or enolate. Also, *esp. Brit.,* **e′no·lise′.** [1935–40; ENOL + -IZE] —**e′no·liz′a·ble,** *adj.* —**e′no·li·za′tion,** *n.*

e·nol·o·gy (ē nol′ə jē), *n.* oenology. —**e·no·log·i·cal** (ē′nl oj′i kəl), *adj.* —**e·nol′o·gist,** *n.*

e·norm (ē nôrm′), *adj. Archaic.* enormous; huge; vast. [1425–75; late ME *enorme* < MF < L *ēnormis,* equiv. to *ē-* E- + *norm*(*a*) NORM + *-is* adj. suffix]

e·nor·mi·ty (i nôr′mi tē), *n., pl.* **-ties 1.** outrageous or heinous character; atrociousness: *the enormity of war crimes.* **2.** something outrageous or heinous, as an offense: *The bombing of the defenseless population was an enormity beyond belief.* **3.** greatness of size, scope, extent, or influence; immensity: *The enormity of such an act of generosity is staggering.* [1425–75; late ME *enormite* < MF < L *ēnormitās.* See ENORM, -TY[2]]
—**Syn. 1.** monstrousness, heinousness. **3.** hugeness, vastness.
—**Usage. 3.** ENORMITY has been in frequent and continuous use in the sense "immensity" since the 18th century: *The enormity of the task was overwhelming.* Some hold that ENORMOUSNESS is the correct word in that sense and that ENORMITY can only mean "outrageousness" or "atrociousness": *The enormity of his offenses appalled the public.* ENORMITY occurs regularly in edited writing with the meanings both of great size and of outrageous or horrifying character, behavior, etc. Many people, however, continue to regard ENORMITY in the sense of great size as nonstandard.

e·nor·mous (i nôr′məs), *adj.* **1.** greatly exceeding the common size, extent, etc.; huge; immense: *an enormous fortune.* **2.** outrageous or atrocious: *enormous wickedness; enormous crimes.* [1525–35; ENORM + -OUS] —**e·nor′mous·ly,** *adv.*
—**Syn. 1.** vast, colossal, gigantic, mammoth, prodigious, stupendous. See **huge.**

e·nor·mous·ness (i nôr′məs nis), *n.* very great or abnormal size, bulk, degree, etc.; immensity; hugeness. [1795–1805; ENORMOUS + -NESS]
—**Usage.** See **enormity.**

E·nos (ē′nəs), *n.* **1.** the son of Seth. Gen. 5:6. **2.** a male given name.

e·no·sis (i nō′sis, ē nō′-; *Gk.* e′nô sēs), *n.* (*sometimes cap.*) a movement for securing the political union of Greece and Cyprus. [1935–40; < ModGk *énōsis,* Gk *hénōsis* union, equiv. to *henō-,* var. s. of *henoûn* to unify (deriv. of *hén,* neut. of *heîs* one) + *-sis* -SIS] —**e·no′sist,** *n.*

e·nough (i nuf′), *adj.* **1.** adequate for the want or need; sufficient for the purpose or to satisfy desire: *enough water; noise enough to wake the dead.* —*pron.* **2.** an adequate quantity or number; sufficiency. —*adv.* **3.** in a quantity or degree that answers a purpose or satisfies a need or desire; sufficiently. **4.** fully or quite: *ready enough.* —*interj.* **5.** (used to express impatience or exasperation): *Enough! I heard you the first time.* [bef. 900; ME *enogh,* OE *genōh;* c. G *genug,* Goth *ganohs,* ON *nōgr;* akin to OE *geneah* it suffices, Skt *naśati* (he) reaches]
—**Syn. 1.** ample. **3.** adequately, amply, reasonably.

e·nounce (i nouns′), *v.t.,* **e·nounced, e·nounc·ing. 1.** to utter or pronounce, as words; enunciate. **2.** to announce, declare, or proclaim. **3.** to state definitely, as a proposition. [1795–1805; E- + (AN)NOUNCE, modeled on F *énoncer* < L *ēnuntiāre* to tell; see ENUNCIATE] —**e·nounce′ment,** *n.*

En·o·vid (en ov′id), *Trademark.* a brand name for a hormonal compound used in medicine in varying doses for ovulation control, adjustment of the menses, severe uterine bleeding, or threatened habitual abortion.

e·now (i nou′; *formerly* i nō′), *adj., adv. Archaic.* enough. [bef. 1050; ME *inow,* OE *genōg* (var. of *genōh* ENOUGH), conflated with ME *inowe,* OE *genōge,* pl. of *genōg* ENOUGH]

en pa·pil·lote (äɴ pᴀ pē yôt′), *French.* (of meat or fish) cooked and served in a wrapping of foil or oiled paper.

en pas·sant (än′ pa sänt′; *Fr.* äɴ pä säɴ′), **1.** (*italics*) *French.* in passing; by the way. **2.** *Chess.* a method by which a pawn that is moved two squares can be captured by an opponent's pawn commanding the square that was passed. [1655–65]

en·phy·tot·ic (en′fī tot′ik), *adj.* **1.** (of a plant disease) regularly affecting but not destroying the plants in a given area. —*n.* **2.** any enphytotic disease. [EN-[2] + Gk *phyt*(*ón*) plant + -OTIC]

en·plane (en plān′), *v.,* **-planed, -plan·ing.** —*v.i.* **1.** to board an airplane: *We enplaned in New York at noon and arrived in Washington an hour later.* —*v.t.* **2.** to allow to board or put on board an airplane: *We will be enplaning passengers shortly.* Also, **emplane.** [1940–45; EN-[1] + PLANE[1]] —**en·plane′ment,** *n.*

en plein air (äɴ ple nᴇʀ′), *French.* in the open air.

en prise (än′ prēz′; *Fr.* äɴ pʀēz′), *Chess.* in line for capture; likely to be captured. [1815–25; < F; see PRIZE[1]]

en′ quad′, *Print.* **1.** a square unit of an area, one en on each side. **2.** a quad having such an area. Cf. **quad**[2] (def. 1). [1900–05]

en·quire (en kwīᵊr′), *v.i., v.t.,* **-quired, -quir·ing.** inquire.

en·quir·y (en kwīᵊr′ē, en′kwə rē), *n., pl.* **-quir·ies.** inquiry.

en·rage (en rāj′), *v.t.,* **-raged, -rag·ing.** to make extremely angry; put into a rage; infuriate: *His supercilious attitude enraged me.* [1490–1500; < MF *enrager.* See EN-[1], RAGE] —**en·rag·ed·ly** (en rā′jid lē, -rājd′-), *adv.* —**en·rage′ment,** *n.*
—**Syn.** anger, inflame, madden. ENRAGE, INCENSE, INFURIATE imply stirring to violent anger. To ENRAGE or TO INFURIATE is to provoke wrath: *They enrage (infuriate) him by their deliberate and continual injustice.* To INCENSE is to inflame with indignation or anger: *to incense a person by making insulting remarks.* —**Ant.** appease, pacify.

en rap·port (än′ ra pôr′, -pōr′, rə-; *Fr.* äɴ ʀᴀ pôʀ′), in sympathy or accord; in agreement; congenial. [< F]

en·rapt (en rapt′), *adj.* rapt; transported; enraptured: *a violinist's enrapt audience.* [1600–10; EN-[1] + RAPT]

en·rap·ture (en rap′chər), *v.t.,* **-tured, -tur·ing.** to move to rapture; delight beyond measure: *We were enraptured by her singing.* [1730–40; EN-[1] + RAPTURE] —**en·rap′tured·ly,** *adv.*
—**Syn.** enthrall, transport, entrance, enchant.

en·rav·ish (en rav′ish), *v.t.* to enrapture. [1590–1600; EN-[1] + RAVISH]

en·reg·is·ter (en rej′ə stər), *v.t.* to register; record. [1515–25; < MF *enregistrer.* See EN-[1], REGISTER] —**en·reg′is·tra′tion,** *n.*

en rè·gle (äɴ ʀe′glᵊ), *French.* in order; according to the rules; correct.

en·rich (en rich′), *v.t.* **1.** to supply with riches, wealth, abundant or valuable possessions, etc.: *Commerce enriches a nation.* **2.** to supply with abundance of anything desirable: *to enrich the mind with knowledge.* **3.** to add greater value or significance to: *Art enriches life.* **4.** to adorn or decorate: *a picture frame enriched with gold.* **5.** to make finer in quality, as by supplying desirable elements or ingredients: *to enrich soil.* **6.** to increase the proportion of a valuable mineral or isotope in (a substance or material): *The fuel was enriched with uranium 235 for the nuclear reactor.* **7.** *Nutrition.* **a.** to restore to (a food) a nutrient that has been lost during an early stage of processing: *to enrich flour with thiamine, iron, niacin, and riboflavin.* **b.** to add vitamins and minerals to (food) to enhance its nutritive value. [1350–1400; ME *enrichen* < OF *enrichir.* See EN-[1], RICH] —**en·rich′er,** *n.* —**en·rich′ing·ly,** *adv.*
—**Syn. 3.** elevate, improve, enhance, endow.

en·rich·ment (en rich′mənt), *n.* **1.** an act of enriching. **2.** the state of being enriched. **3.** something that enriches: *the enrichments of education and travel.* [1620–30; ENRICH + -MENT]

En·ri·co (en rē′kō; *It.* en ʀē′kô), *n.* a male given name: Italian form of **Henry.**

En·ri·qui·llo (en′ri kē′ō; *Sp.* en′ʀē kē′yô), *n.* **Lake,** a saltwater lake, below sea level, in the SW Dominican Republic.

en·robe (en rōb′), *v.t.,* **-robed, -rob·ing.** to dress; attire: *The king was enrobed in velvet.* [1585–95; EN-[1] + ROBE] —**en·rob′er,** *n.*

en·rol (en rōl′), *v.t., v.i.,* **-rolled, -rol·ling.** enroll.

en·roll (en rōl′), *v.t.* **1.** to write the name of (a person) in a roll or register; place upon a list; register: *It took two days to enroll the new students.* **2.** to enlist (oneself). **3.** to put in a record; record: *to enroll the minutes of a meeting; to enroll the great events of history.* **4.** to roll or wrap up: *fruit enrolled in tissue paper.* **5.** *Naut.* to document (a U.S. vessel) by issuing a certificate of enrollment. —*v.i.* **6.** to enroll oneself: *He enrolled in college last week.* [1300–50; ME *enrollen* < OF *enroller.* See EN-[1], ROLL] —**en·roll′er,** *n.*

enrolled′ bill′, *U.S. Govt.* a copy of a bill passed by both houses of Congress, signed by their presiding officers, and sent to the President for signature. Cf. **engrossed bill.** [1780–90, *Amer.*]

en·roll·ee (en rō lē′, -rō′lē), *n.* a person enrolled, in a class, school, course of study, etc. [ENROLL + -EE]

en·roll·ment (en rōl′mənt), *n.* **1.** the act or process of enrolling. **2.** the state of being enrolled. **3.** the number of persons enrolled, as for a course or in a school. Also, **en·rol′ment.** [1525–35; ENROLL + -MENT]

en·root (en ro͞ot′, -ro͝ot′), *v.t.* **1.** to fix by the root. **2.** to attach or place securely; implant deeply. [1480–90; EN-[1] + ROOT[1]]

en route (än ro͞ot′, en; *Fr.* äɴ ʀo͞ot′), on the way: *The plane crashed en route from Cairo to Athens.* [1770–80; < F]

ens (enz, ens), *n., pl.* **en·ti·a** (en′shē ə, -tē ə), *Metaphys.* an existing or real thing; an entity. [< L *ēns,* prp. of *esse* to be]

Ens., Ensign.

en·sam·ple (en sam′pəl), *n. Archaic.* example. [1200–50; ME < OF, var. (*en-* EN- r. *es-*) of *essample* < OF < L *exemplum* EXAMPLE]

en·san·guine (en sang′gwin), *v.t.,* **-guined, -guin·ing.** to stain or cover with or as with blood: *a flag ensanguined with the blood of battle.* [1660–70; EN-[1] + SANGUINE]

En·sche·de (en′sᴋʜə dā′), *n.* a city in E Netherlands. 144,346.

en·sconce (en skons′), *v.t.,* **-sconced, -sconc·ing. 1.** to settle securely or snugly: *I found her in the library, ensconced in an armchair.* **2.** to cover or shelter; hide securely: *He ensconced himself in the closet in order to eavesdrop.* [1580–90; EN-[1] + SCONCE[2]]

en·scroll (en skrōl′), *v.t.* **1.** to commemorate or record in a permanent manner, by or as if by inscribing on parchment. **2.** to write or inscribe on a scroll. Also, **inscroll.** [1905–10; EN-[1] + SCROLL]

en·sem·ble (än säm′bəl, -sämb′; *Fr.* äɴ säɴ′blᵊ), *n., pl.* **-sem·bles** (-säm′bəlz, -sämbz′; *Fr.* -säɴ′blᵊ). **1.** all the parts of a thing taken together, so that each part is considered only in relation to the whole. **2.** the entire costume of an individual, esp. when all the parts are in harmony: *She was wearing a beautiful ensemble by one of the French designers.* **3.** a set of furniture. **4.** *Music.* **a.** the united performance of an entire group of singers, musicians, etc. **b.** the group so performing: *a string ensemble.* **5.** a group of supporting entertainers, as actors, dancers, and singers, in a theatrical production. [1740–50; < F: together < L *insimul,* equiv. to *in-* IN-[2] + *simul* together; see SIMULTANEOUS]
—**Syn. 1.** totality, entirety, aggregate.

ensem′ble act′ing, an approach to acting that aims for a unified effect achieved by all members of a cast working together on behalf of the play, rather than emphasizing individual performances. [1925–30]

En·se·na·da (en′se nä′t͟hä; *Eng.* en′sə nä′də), *n.* a seaport in N Lower California, in NW Mexico. 113,320.

en·se pe·tit pla·ci·dam sub li·ber·ta·te qui·e·tem (en′se pe′tit plä′ki däm′ so͝ob lē′beʀ tä′te kwē-ā′tem; *Eng.* en′sē pē′tit plas′i dam′ sub lib′ər tā′tē kwī ē′tem), *Latin.* by the sword she seeks quiet peace under liberty: motto of Massachusetts.

en·sep·ul·cher (en sep′əl kər), *v.t.* to place in a sepulcher; entomb. [1810–20; EN-[1] + SEPULCHER]

en·serf (en sûrf′), *v.t.* to make a serf of; place in bondage. [1880–85; EN-[1] + SERF]

en·sheathe (en shēt͟h′), *v.t.,* **-sheathed, -sheath·ing.** to enclose in or as in a sheath; sheathe. Also, **en·sheath′,** (en shēth′), **insheathe, insheath.** [1585–95; EN-[1] + SHEATHE]

en·shrine (en shrīn′), *v.t.,* **-shrined, -shrin·ing. 1.** to enclose in or as in a shrine: *His love for her is enshrined forever in his poetry.* **2.** to cherish as sacred: *The memory of our friendship will be enshrined in my heart.* Also, **inshrine.** [1575–85; EN-[1] + SHRINE] —**en·shrine′·ment,** *n.*

en·shroud (en shroud′), *v.t.* to shroud; conceal. [1575–85; EN-[1] + SHROUD]

en·si·form (en′sə fôrm′), *adj.* sword-shaped; xiphoid. [1535–45; < L *ēnsi*(*s*) sword + -FORM]

en·sign (en′sīn; *Mil.* en′sən), *n.* **1.** a flag or banner, as a military or naval standard used to indicate nationality. **2.** a badge of office or authority, as heraldic arms. **3.** a sign, token, or emblem: *the dove, an ensign of peace.* **4.** *U.S. Navy and Coast Guard.* the lowest commissioned officer, ranking next below a lieutenant, junior grade, and equal to a second lieutenant in the Army. **5.** *Archaic.* standard-bearer (def. 1). [1325–75; ME *ensigne* < OF *enseigne* < L *insignia;* see INSIGNIA] —**en′sign·ship′, en′sign·cy,** *n.*
—**Syn. 1.** pennant, streamer.

en′sign staff′, a staff at the stern of a vessel at which the ensign is flown. Also called **poop staff.** [1700–10]

en·si·lage (en′sə lij), *n., v.,* **-laged, -lag·ing.** —*n.* **1.** the preservation of green fodder in a silo or pit. **2.** fodder preserved. —*v.t.* **3.** ensile. [1875–80; < F; see ENSILE, -AGE]

en·sile (en sīl′, en′sīl), *v.t.,* **-siled, -sil·ing. 1.** to preserve (green fodder) in a silo. **2.** to make into ensilage. [1880–85; < F *ensiler* < Sp *ensilar,* equiv. to *en-* EN-[1] + *-silar,* v. deriv. of *silo* SILO] —**en·si′la·bil′i·ty,** *n.*

-ensis a Latin adjectival suffix meaning "pertaining to," "originating in," used in modern Latin scientific coinages, esp. derivatives of placenames: *canadensis; carolinensis.* [< L *-ēnsis;* cf. -ESE]

en·sky (en skī′), *v.t.,* **-skied** or **-skyed, -sky·ing.** to place in or as if in the heavens; exalt. [1595–1605; EN-[1] + SKY]

en·slave (en slāv′), *v.t.,* **-slaved, -slav·ing.** to make a slave of; reduce to slavery: *His drug addiction has completely enslaved him.* [1635–45; EN-[1] + SLAVE] —**en·slave′ment,** *n.* —**en·slav′er,** *n.*
—**Syn.** enchain, shackle; control, dominate. —**Ant.** free, liberate, release.

en·snare (en snâr′), *v.t.,* **-snared, -snar·ing.** to capture in, or involve as in, a snare: *to be ensnared by lies; to ensnare birds.* Also, **insnare.** [1585–95; EN-[1] + SNARE[1]] —**en·snare′ment,** *n.* —**en·snar′er,** *n.* —**en·snar′ing·ly,** *adv.*
—**Syn.** entrap, entangle, enmesh. —**Ant.** release.

en·snarl (en snärl′), *v.t.* to entangle in or as in a snarl. [1585–95; EN[1]- + SNARL[2]]

CONCISE PRONUNCIATION KEY: act, cāpe, dâre, pärt; set, ēqual; if, īce; ox, ōver, ôrder, oil, bo͝ok, bo͞ot, out; up, ûrge; child; sing; shoe; thin, t͟hat; zh as in *treasure.* ə = *a* as in *alone,* *e* as in *system,* *i* as in *easily,* *o* as in *gallop,* *u* as in *circus;* ᵊ as in *fire* (fīᵊr), *hour* (ouᵊr). l and n can serve as syllabic consonants, as in *cradle* (krād′l), and *button* (but′n). See the full key inside the front cover.

Dictionary page from *The Random House Unabridged Dictionary,* 2d ed. (New York: Random House, 1993).

C. Use your dictionary to look up any words you don't understand in this chapter. Keep a list of these words and study them often.

I. Philosophy of American Education

A. The following is a list of some basic principles from which the American education system has evolved. These principles have been established by several educational philosophers throughout the years. Match each principle with the goals that are present in modern American education.

Principle

1. ___ The schools and religion are kept separate.
2. ___ All children are allowed to attend school.
3. ___ The federal government does not have control over education.
4. ___ The schools should develop the national unity and character of their students.
5. ___ Children should learn how to develop their own intellectual and creative abilities.

Modern Goals

a. Schools give students a sense of national and community awareness.
b. Students concentrate on solving problems instead of memorizing facts.
c. Public schools are financed by local/state governments.
d. Schools are expected to meet the needs of all children, regardless of ability or background.
e. Public religious prayer is forbidden in public schools.

B. Summarize the educational philosophy of your country. What similarities are there between the United States and your country? Differences?

II. The Organization of American Schools

A. Let's now look at the structure of schools. How many hours a day did you go to elementary school? junior high school? high school? What subjects did you study during each period? Compare your answers with other students in your class.

B. Read the following selection.

STRUCTURE OF AMERICAN SCHOOLS

The American school system includes public, private, and parochial schools. Public schools are funded through state and local taxes; students at private schools, in contrast, usually have to pay tuition to attend the school, and they often are required to wear uniforms. Although the administration of private and public schools is different, and many schools are experimenting with different programs, the structure of many schools is relatively the same.

Compulsory education in the United States begins around age 6. Children can quit school around age 16 in more than half of the states, but most states discourage this by requiring parental permission. In addition, it is very difficult to get a job in the United States without a high school diploma or the G.E.D. (general equivalency diploma).

The first year of required education in most elementary school systems is kindergarten. The rules vary among states, but in general, children are approximately the same age (5–6) when they begin kindergarten. Prior to kindergarten, some parents choose to send their children to nursery school (preschool), but this is not required. Children are introduced to a social environment and learn basic skills of coordination in nursery school. In kindergarten, children go to school for half a day (either morning or afternoon), and, in addition to learning how to interact socially, they begin some preliminary work in basic skills, such as reading and writing.

Elementary school usually includes grades 1–5 or 1–6. Grades 6–8 (or 7–9) are often housed in a different building than the lower grades. These schools are called either middle schools or junior high schools. Students in elementary schools (also called grade or grammar schools) usually meet with the same teacher in the same room during the day. Basic subjects such as math, social studies, science, and sometimes art and music are covered.

Between the ages of 12 and 14, American students attend junior high school or middle school. This period is usually considered part of American secondary education. Junior high school students take certain compulsory courses that are included in the curriculum of that state. For the most part, these courses include English, general math, physical education, general science, and social studies. Students can also take elective courses such as foreign language, manual arts, or home economics.

High school usually begins with either 9th or 10th grade. Its curriculum can include either college preparatory or vocational courses, depending on the interests of the student. College prep courses include English, math, science, and foreign languages. Vocational courses include technical or trade subjects, such as automobile mechanics, woodworking, home economics, or drafting. Students at all levels (freshman, sophomore, junior, senior) are also able to choose several elective courses.

Extracurricular activities (student council, sports, band, choir, language clubs, etc.) are very popular among some high school students. Participation in extracurricular activities is considered an important part of the socialization of the students. The purpose of the activities is to help students develop interests outside of their academic courses and to help develop a feeling of "school spirit." The clubs usually support themselves by raising money through fund-raising activities.

The academic year for most states in the United States lasts from late August or early September until May or June. It may be longer in some states, depending on the length of vacations and the number of required school days. Some schools divide the year into quarters (three sessions) and others use the semester system (two sessions). Classes are held Monday through Friday with a variation on hours between 7:30 and 3:30. Students involved in extracurricular activities usually do not return home until evening.

Even though there may be some variation in the structure of elementary, junior high, and high schools in the United States, most states follow the above-mentioned pattern. There are several experimental schools, however, that are addressing the problems in American education and have started to break with many of the traditions.

C. Using the information from the reading, fill in the appropriate information in the chart.

Age	Grade(s)	School	Possible Subjects/Activities
3–4	—		social skills basic coordination activities
5–6	kindergarten	part of elementary school	
6–11			
12–14		junior high school	
15–18			

D. Recognizing the relationship between words in a text increases comprehension. Look at the following sentence from the reading:

The school year in the United States lasts from late August or early September until May or June. *It* may be longer in some states, depending on the length of vacations and the number of required school days.

What does *It* refer to?

Reference Words: Pronouns

An author will often make use of references, words or phrases that refer to a previous (and sometimes following) idea in the text. This technique is used to avoid unnecessary repetition in his/her writing. A key skill for English learners is to recognize these reference words and determine the words or ideas they refer to. The first step is to be aware of the different referencing techniques the author uses. One technique is pronoun reference.

Use pronouns to indicate the previously stated noun or noun phrase:

a. Subject and object pronouns:
   Junior high schools are very similar to high schools. *Students* are allowed to take some elective courses, and *they* also change rooms and teachers throughout the day.
b. Possessive pronouns:
   Several American high school students are very busy with *their* part-time jobs and extracurricular activities.
c. Demonstrative pronouns (this/that, these, those, such):
   The students *call their English professor by her first name. This informality* is common among some American university professors.

E. Read the following sentences. Identify the words or phrases that the italicized words refer to.

Example:

   Compulsory education in the United States begins around age 6. Children can quit school around age 16 in more than half of the states, but most states discourage *this* by requiring parental permission.
   this   quitting school

1. Prior to kindergarten, some parents choose to send their children to nursery school (preschool), but *this* is not required.
   this

2. In kindergarten, children go to school for half a day (either morning or afternoon), and, in addition to learning how to interact socially, *they* also begin some preliminary work in basic skills such as reading and writing.
   they

3. Between the ages of 12 and 14, American students attend junior high school or middle school. *This period* is usually considered part of American secondary education.
   This period

4. Junior high school students take certain compulsory courses that are included in the curriculum of that state. For the most part, *these* courses include English, general math, physical education, general science, and social studies.
   these

5. High school usually begins with either 9th or 10th grade. *Its* curriculum can include either college preparatory or vocational courses, depending on the interests of the student.
   Its

F. As mentioned in "Structure of American Schools," uniforms are not required in public schools in the United States. Several private schools, however, require all students to wear uniforms. Some students, teachers, and parents believe that there are several advantages and disadvantages to a dress code. Look at the list of advantages and disadvantages that Tom Drenegoski, principal of a parochial school, proposed. Which of the following are advantages (A) to requiring uniforms and which are disadvantages (D)?

1. ____ Students would be well dressed.

2. ____ Parents would have less trouble finding clothes for their children.

3. ____ Students don't like uniforms.

4. ____ School clothes would be less expensive.

5. ____ Students would lose a sense of individuality.

6. ____ Students wouldn't have competition for designer clothes.

7. ____ Students in schools that don't require uniforms might tease students who wear uniforms.

8. ____ There would be a perception of a military image, of soldiers in uniform.

(Information from Dana Yvette George, "The Uniform Solution," *Lansing State Journal*, January 25, 1994, 1+.)

G. Get into groups and imagine that you are members of the student council (student government). You have been asked by your fellow students to convince the school board to eliminate uniforms. Read the arguments given by the school board and decide how you would refute (prove they are mistaken or argue against) them.

1. Uniforms are less expensive.
   Refutation: *Students can't use the uniforms outside of school like regular clothes.*

2. Parents have less trouble finding clothes for their children with the uniform policy.
   Refutation:

3. Students do not have to compete for designer clothing.
   Refutation:

4. Every student is well dressed.
   Refutation:

H. Using the form provided, write a letter to Diane Sherwood, the school principal of Wilkins Junior High School, and persuade her to adopt or not adopt a uniform policy.

September 16, 19—

Principal Diane Sherwood
Wilkins Junior High School
1651 Touhy Ave.
Justice, IL 60973

Sincerely,

III. Enrollment in American Schools

A. Listen to the following sentence that comes from a lecture about enrollment in American schools. What do you think your notes should
look like?

    a. The number of 3-year-olds enrolled in school increased from 13
        percent in 1970 to 28 percent in 1992
    b. # of 3 yr. olds enrolled in school↑ from 13% in '70 to 28% in '92

(Information from *Digest of Education Statistics, 1995.* [Washington,
D.C.: United States Dept. of Health, Education, and Welfare, Education Division, National Center for Education Statistics, Office of Educational Research and Development, 1995]).

Using Abbreviations and Symbols

There are many situations you may find yourself in where you want to take notes on a talk you are listening to. The challenge in taking notes is to (1) try and understand the organization of the talk in order to organize your notes; (2) identify the important details; and (3) write fast enough to record these details. This is a difficult job in a first language and a more difficult job in a second language. Therefore, it is important that you be patient and understand that note taking is a skill that requires a lot of practice.

To help you take notes more quickly, you can use several note-taking symbols and abbreviations. There are no "rules" for how to abbreviate words, or make them shorter. People all use symbols and abbreviate words a little differently, but there are some guidelines that you should keep in mind:

1. Use standard symbols (see exercise that follows)
2. Shorten dates (September 2, 1968 → 9/2/68)
3. Use the first syllable and/or first few letters of the second (history → hist)
4. Omit vowels (develop → dvlp)
5. Omit prepositions and articles (a, of, the, on, . . .)
6. After first use, abbreviate proper nouns (Scholastic Aptitude Test → SAT)

B. Match the note-taking symbols on the left with their meaning. Write the appropriate letter in the blank.

1. ___ =   a. therefore

2. ___ <   b. approximately

3. ___ >   c. increase

4. ___ &   d. for example

5. ___ w/   e. without

6. ___ ↑   f. less than

7. ___ →   g. with

8. ___ e.g.   h. equals, is

9. ___ ↓   i. more than

10. ___ ≅   j. number

11. ___ ∴   k. decrease

12. ___ #   l. between

13. ___ w/o   m. cause

14. ___ ~   n. and

C. Rewrite the following sentences using abbreviations and note-taking symbols.

Example:

Elementary school enrollment increased by 13 percent between 1985 and 1992. (John W. Wright, ed. *The Universal Almanac 1995.* [Kansas City: Andrews and McMeel, 1994])

Elem. school enroll. ↑ *by 13% ~ '85 & '92.*

1. Between 1980 and 1990, the number of persons 25 and older enrolled in college increased more than 34 percent. (*Digest of Education Statistics, 1995* [Washington, D.C.: U.S. Dept. of Health, Education, and Welfare, Education Division, National Center for Education Statistics, Office of Educational Research and Development, 1995])

2. The sources of money for public schools vary among the states. For example, in the state of New Hampshire, 86.6 percent of the money for schools comes from the local school districts and 7.9 percent comes from state taxes. The rest of the money comes from

federal and private sources. In New Mexico, however, 11.3 percent comes from the local districts and 73.7 percent of the money comes from the state, with the rest coming from federal and private sources. (*Digest of Education Statistics, 1995* [Washington, D.C.: U.S. Dept. of Health, Education, and Welfare, Education Division, National Center for Education Statistics, Office of Educational Research and Development, 1995])

3. The cost of tuition and required fees for public four-year universities increased from an average of $427 in 1970 to $2,352 in 1993. This is less than private universities, which charge approximately $10,393 for tuition and fees per year. (*The World Almanac and Book of Facts: 1995* [Mahwah, N.J.: Funk and Wagnalls Corporation, 1994])

D. Listen to the entire lecture. On a separate sheet of paper, take notes using note-taking symbols and abbreviations.

E. Listen to the lecture again and answer the following questions using your lecture notes.

1. T / F California and Texas enroll fewer than 1,000 students per district.
2. T / F There are approximately 43,000,000 students in American public schools.
3. T / F About 8 million American students attend private schools.
4. T / F The United States has over 50,000 school districts.
5. T / F New Jersey spends more money per student than any other state.

IV. American Higher Education

A. In groups, brainstorm everything you know about American colleges and universities. Write these words, phrases, and sentences on a separate sheet of paper.

B. Use these words in the following sentences.

funded	affiliations	plentiful
interchanged	postsecondary	prior to
plentiful		obtain

1. Universities are _____ in large urban areas in every American city.
2. Private and religious institutions can be very expensive because they do not receive the same type of funding that public schools do, although they may _____ some money from the state for certain programs.
3. Students pay tuition at public universities, but those who have resided in the state for a certain period of time _____ beginning classes do not pay as much as nonresidents.
4. Some private schools have religious _____ (Protestant, Roman Catholic, and Jewish), but it is usually not necessary to be a member of that particular religion to attend the school.
5. The words "college" and "university" are often _____, but it is generally understood that a university can offer graduate degrees as well.
6. This broad range of choices in _____ education provides every student with an opportunity to attain his or her personal and occupational goals.
7. Public universities are owned and _____ by the states in which they are located.

C. Read the following article about higher education. Ignore the blank lines in the article for now. We will work with these in the next activity.

HIGHER EDUCATION IN THE UNITED STATES

The higher education system in the United States is one of the largest in the world.___ ___ This broad range of choices in postsecondary education provides every student with an opportunity to attain his or her personal and occupational goals. Universities are plentiful in large urban areas in every American city. However, if a person prefers a more rural setting, there are also hundreds of colleges located away from the large cities.

Higher education in the United States includes any program of study at two-year junior colleges, four-year colleges and universities, and graduate schools.___ ___ The words "college" and "university" are often interchanged, but it is generally understood that a university can offer graduate degrees as well. These degrees can be quite specialized, such as a Master of Arts in a particular subject or even doctorate degrees.

American colleges and universities may be public, private, or religious. Public universities are owned and funded by the states in which they are located. Students pay tuition at public universities, but those who have resided in the state for a certain period of time prior to beginning classes do not pay as much as nonresidents.___ These costs, however, depend on the size, location, reputation, etc. of the university.

Private and religious institutions can be very expensive because they do not receive the same type of funding that public schools do, although they may obtain some money from the state for certain programs. Some American private universities are considered the best in the nation, if not in the world, but the costs of these schools are very high.___ Some private schools have religious affiliations (Protestant, Roman Catholic, and Jewish), but it is usually not necessary to be a member of that particular religion to attend the school. In fact, some of the affiliations are purely historical.

Last, there are also some technical institutions that are privately owned, like businesses.___ The training is very specialized, and the goals of the student are specifically related to a particular occupation.

D. Of the following two sentences about American higher education, which is easier to understand and more convincing?

1. The average cost of a four-year college is expensive. It increases each year.
2. The average cost of a four-year college is expensive. Each year, it increases at least 8%.

Supporting Details

You already know that most writing in English is organized from general to specific. In a paragraph, the most general statement is usually the topic sentence. The topic sentence is followed by specific statements, which are called supporting details. Supporting details are very important for writing because they help the reader understand your main point more easily, and they convince the reader about the point you are making. Supporting details can be facts or statistics, examples, personal experiences, observations, or statements by authorities on the subject.

E. The following statements are all specific details about higher education in the United States. Go back to the reading. Every place there is a blank line (___), a supporting detail(s) is needed. Write the number(s) of the following sentences on the correct line(s) in the reading. If there is one line, choose one of the sentences. If there are two, choose two, etc.

1. Students can choose among large research institutions with over 25,000 students or smaller colleges with fewer than 1,000 students.
2. A nonresident student may pay as much as 50 or 60% more than a resident student.
3. The average cost of tuition, fees, and room and board at private four-year colleges was $15,128 in 1993–94.
4. There are over 3,300 different colleges and universities in the United States.
5. Junior colleges, most of which are called community colleges, offer the Associate of Arts or the Associate of Science degrees (A.A. or A.S.).
6. Four-year colleges grant undergraduate bachelor's degrees (B.A. or B.S.).
7. These technical institutes offer two-year programs in such fields as automotive engineering, business, and electronics.

F. Now answer the following questions about the reading on pages 83–84.

1. Why do you think private colleges and universities are more expensive than public ones?

2. What degrees do junior colleges offer? four-year colleges?

3. What is the difference between a college and a university? Do you think that both words are used to describe postsecondary education?

4. Why do you think that tuition for nonresidents is more expensive at public schools?

5. Would you rather attend a large public university or a small private university? Why?

G. Many abbreviations and initials are used in American universities. The following are abbreviations that are often used on college campuses. Try to guess what each abbreviation represents and then write each abbreviation in the appropriate column.

Courses	*Degrees*	*Grades/Exams*
econ. = economics		

A.A.	GMAT	Ph.D.	econ.	bio.
A.S.	prereq	poli. sci.	GPA	SAT
ACT	psych.	M.A.	P.E.	B.S.

H. Scan the course schedule that follows in order to answer the questions.

1. What class is offered at 1:00 on Mondays, Wednesdays, and Fridays?
2. Which course is the only one available for a student who has to take night classes?
3. Which course does Professor Kountz teach?
4. Who teaches the honor section of Anthropology 100?
5. When does Anthropology 341 meet?

Western Michigan University

Course	Description			Credit
Call No. Days	Hours	Location	Instructor	

-Anthropology-
(Call 387-3639 for an appointment)

ANTH 100	**Human Origins**			**3.0**
11972 MWF	1000-1050am	Moore 00120	McGowan	
***** MWF	1200-1250pm	Knaus 03760	Helling	

This section is for honor students only. You must obtain call number from Lee Honors College course booklet or Lee Honors College.

ANTH 110	**Lost Worlds/Archeology**			**3.0**
56103 TR	800-920am	Moore 00116	Bray	
58338 TR	200-320pm	Moore 00116	Bray	

ANTH 120	**Peoples of the World**			**3.0**
21993 MWF	1000-1050am	Sangn 02303	O'Gorman	
60687 TR	1100-1220pm	Moore 00116	Arensbach	
46361 TR	1230-150pm	Wood 00170	Matthews	
19670 T	630-900pm	Wood 00170	Young	
46349 TR	930-1050am	Sangn 02302	Kuiper	

ANTH 140	**Anthropology in Action**			**3.0**
48766 TR	930-1050am	Moore 00116	Hutton	

ANTH 210	**Intro to Archeology**			**3.0**
38803 TR	930-1050am	Moore 00120	Hageman	

ANTH 240	**Principles of Cult Anthropology**			**3.0**
29230 MWF	100-150pm	Moore 00116	Lestarcyzk	

ANTH 310	**Environmental Archeology**			**3.0**
56112 TR	1100-1220pm	Moore 00120	Alkhas	

ANTH 339	**Cultures of Latin America**			**3.0**
60496 MWF	900-950am	Knaus 03760	Kountz	

ANTH 341	**Cultures of Africa**			**3.0**
60676 TR	330-450pm	Moore 00120	Belczak	

ANTH 342	**Cultures of Mid East**			**3.0**
56130 TR	1100-1220pm	Knaus 03770	Flood	

From the *Fall 1995 Directory of Classes*, anthropology section, Western Michigan University.

I. Get into groups and discuss the following questions.

1. Do you have any special admissions programs in your country for students who are not academically ready for college?
2. Do you think that everyone should be given a chance to study at a university?
3. Do you think that students should receive college credit for the remedial (catch-up) courses that they have to take during the first year?

J. Read the following excerpt from a university catalog.

Special Admission Programs

ALPHA PROGRAM

The Alpha Program is a limited admission program that seeks to provide the opportunity for college level work with academic assistance and support. The program provides academic advising and counseling, alerts students to tutoring services, and requires attendance at skill building workshops.

Consideration is given to those students who do not meet WMU's regular admissions criteria but who have demonstrated the potential for college level work. From this pool, the University's Office of Admissions and Orientation will select those students who appear to have the best chance for success. Interested students should follow regular admissions procedures; the Office of Admissions and Orientation will notify those eligible for further consideration as Alpha students.

Admission to the Alpha Program is on a one year probationary basis. Selected students, and their parents, must sign a program contract accepting conditions of admission. These include:

1. Enrollment in WMU's University Curriculum (UNV);
2. Attendance at Freshman Orientation;
3. Meeting with the Alpha/UNV Orientation advisor to schedule classes.
4. Enrollment in 100 and/or 200 level courses during the freshman year;
5. Registration for not more than 14 credit hours each semester during the freshman year;
6. Maintenance of a minimum 2.0 ("C") grade point average while at WMU;
7. Attendance at regularly scheduled skill building workshops; and
8. Meeting with the Alpha/UNV advisor throughout each semester of the freshman year.

Before the end of each semester, students' grades and progress are reviewed by an Alpha/UNV advisor. All students who have met the contract conditions will be permitted to continue in the program. Those who complete the terms of the probationary year will be eligible to continue their college work in good standing.

From the *1993–1995 Western Michigan University, Undergraduate Catalog*, Alpha Program section, Western Michigan University.

K. Imagine that you are an Alpha/UNV Orientation advisor and it is your job to talk with Alpha students at the end of their freshman year. You need to confirm that the student has met each of the conditions of admission. What are the questions that you should ask?

1. Are you enrolled in the WMU University Curriculum?

2.

3.

4.

5.

6.

7.

8.

V. Problems in American Education

A. Before we learn about a few problems that American education is facing, brainstorm some possible problems that you think are common to educational systems in countries all over the world.

B. During the 1980s, many educators started to study the problems in the American education system. Former President George Bush proposed several goals for the new century that are referred to as the Goals 2000 (*Goals 2000: A Progress Report* [Washington, D.C.: U.S. Department of Education, 1995]). The following is one of those goals:

> By the year 2000, every school will promote partnerships that will increase parental involvement and participation in promoting the social, emotional, and academic growth of children.

Now read another version of the same goal. Does this version say the same thing? How is this version different?

All schools, before the end of this century, will encourage relationships that help parents become more involved and participate in their children's social, emotional, and academic growth.

Paraphrasing

Paraphrasing is a process by which writers express someone else's meaning in their own words. Paraphrasing is a very helpful tool when you are trying to remember new concepts or vocabulary that are difficult; it is much easier to remember them if you can say them in your own words!

Paraphrasing other people's words and ideas is a very difficult skill. You must not only understand the meaning, but you must also rewrite the language yet keep its original meaning. Paraphrasing requires a great deal of practice and skill.

How to Paraphrase

1. Read the passage very carefully to make sure that you understand the meaning.
2. Put the material aside and then write in your own words what you remember.
3. Check your writing against the original by rereading the passage to make sure that you have
   a. conveyed the same meaning;
   b. kept your paraphrase about the same length; and
   c. written the paraphrase in your own style of writing.

Techniques for Paraphrasing

1. Change the *grammatical structure:*
   a. join short sentences or break up long ones;
   b. change the active verbs to passive or the passive verbs to active; and
   c. change the word order, especially of adverbs.
2. Change the *vocabulary* to more common synonyms/expressions and simpler phrases. However, you should *not* change technical vocabulary (global economy), proper names (former President George Bush), or numbers/statistics (90%, 2000).

C. Read some of the other Goals 2000. Then, paraphrase them *in your own words.*

    1. The high school graduation rate will increase to at least 90 percent.

    2. American students will be first in the world in mathematics and science achievement.

    3. Every adult American will be literate and will possess the knowledge and skills necessary to compete in a global economy and exercise the rights and responsibilities of citizenship.

    4. Every school in the United States will be free of drugs, violence, and the unauthorized presence of firearms and alcohol and will offer a disciplined environment conducive to learning.

    5. The nation's teaching force will have access to programs for the continued improvement of their professional skills and the opportunity to acquire the knowledge and skills needed to instruct and prepare all American students for the next century.

D. Now look at a list of problems that have been cited in the past two decades regarding the American education system. Which of the Goals 2000 (1–5) in Activity C do you think addresses each one of these problems?

a. Every school day, 135,000 students bring guns to school. (Gerald Leinwand, *Public Education*, New York: Facts on File, 1992)

b. Teachers in many cities do not receive the support necessary to continue their education and development.

c. In 1994–95, there were 73 graduates for every 100 high school students. (*Digest of Education Statistics, 1995* [Washington, D.C.: U.S. Dept. of Health, Education, and Welfare, Education Division, National Center for Education Statistics, Office of Educational Research and Development, 1995])

d. A 1983 study reported that 23 million American adults are functionally illiterate—they cannot perform simple, daily reading/writing tasks (United States, The National Commission on Excellence in Education, *A Nation at Risk*, Washington, D.C.: GPO, 1983)

e. The United States recently ranked 13th out of 14 developed countries in math achievement (*Newsweek*, September 11, 1995, 12)

E. In small groups, choose one of the problems/goals matching from Activity D and brainstorm possible ways to solve this problem.

VI. Values Application

A. Read the following letter that an international student wrote to her friend describing her first year of high school as an exchange student in the United States. Ignore the numbers for now.

Dear Brea,

Hi! How are you? I just finished my first semester here. So far, my junior year abroad has been fantastic! I have made a lot of new friends, and I'm really glad that I decided to spend a year here, although I am surprised at the differences between the schools here and the ones at home.

The first day I walked into the high school, I was shocked. I knew I wouldn't have to wear a uniform, but when my math teacher walked into the room wearing jeans, I couldn't believe it! (1).

Another big difference is that I was able to choose all my courses. Of course, we all have to take some science, math, and English courses, but since I really like biology more than chemistry, I signed up for microbiology (2). I did really well on my last exam in that class. When the teacher returned them, I noticed that nobody in the class showed each other their scores. I guess students like to keep their grades to themselves here (3).

A lot of students in my math class are seniors, so they're starting to look at colleges for next year. Many of them are working part-time now to save money for college (4). Most of them do not know what they want to major in, but the counselors here have encouraged them to wait and specialize during their second or third year of college. Many of them took tests called the ACT and the SAT last month. Compared to our country, it seems that anyone can go to almost any college they want because here the students don't have to pass an entrance exam (5). In fact, my host brother, who has had a difficult time in high school and has not received very good grades, will be able to attend college by taking some special courses during his first year (6).

I hope you're enjoying school too. I miss you very much, and I'm looking forward to seeing you next June.

Your friend,
Jina

B. Reread the numbered sentences in the letter and decide which value from chapter 1 is reflected in each statement.

1. _____

2. _____

3. _____

4. _____

5. _____

6. _____

Chapter 5

Earning a Living: The American Workplace

Read the following statements. Write a *T* if you think the statement is true, or an *F* if you think it is false. As you study this chapter, you will discover whether these statements are true or false. When you finish the chapter, return to this page and check your answers to see if they are correct.

1. ____ Fewer farm jobs, as a result of industrialization, forced Americans to move to bigger cities.
2. ____ Women generally receive six weeks paid maternity leave in the United States.
3. ____ Workers in smaller companies usually get fewer benefits than employees in larger companies.
4. ____ Universities often offer free or reduced tuition to the children of professors who work there.
5. ____ Many American workers get three weeks paid vacation.

6. ____ On the average, farmers made less than $300.00 per week in 1993.
7. ____ Business meetings usually start about 15–30 minutes after the scheduled time.
8. ____ American workers tend to be more competitive than cooperative.

A Look Behind/A Look Ahead

In chapter 4, we studied about the American education system. We learned about the philosophy and structure of the system. We also explored American higher education and some problems that education faces. We discovered that individualism is emphasized in American schools as students are able to choose many of their own courses as early as junior high school.

In this chapter we will look at the American workplace and further study the American values that are present in everyday living. Some aspects of the workplace will be discussed, including different types of occupations, sexist and nonsexist job titles, and the earnings and benefits of several different occupations. As with the other chapters, significant American values in the workplace will also be explored.

To the Student

After completing this chapter, you will be able to

1. classify occupations into categories;
2. distinguish between sexist and nonsexist job titles;
3. identify earnings and benefits of several different occupations;
4. analyze the idea of cooperation/competition in the American workplace;
5. understand how Americans view time in business;
6. identify values in the American workforce.

After completing this chapter, return to this page and assess your own achievement of these objectives.

Vocabulary Development

In chapter 3, we learned about suffixes, which can indicate the different parts of speech, such as nouns, verbs, adjectives, and adverbs. In the dictionary, these forms are often listed as undefined at the end of the definition. The accompanying chart lists some of the vocabulary words you will encounter in this chapter. Complete the chart, keeping in mind that the word formation may not be the same for all the words and that some boxes may remain empty.

Noun	Verb	Adjective	Adverb
	classify		
employer, employee			
			collaboratively
		industrialized	
		qualified	
	cooperate		
			efficiently
benefit			
		managerial	

Write any other new vocabulary words from this chapter.

I. Different Types of Occupations in the United States

In industrialized societies, there are a wide variety of occupations. There are several different ways to classify most occupations, but many American jobs are categorized based on the amount of skill or training that is necessary to perform the job as well as where the work is performed.

A. Scan the following reading passage and write the four different categories of occupations that Americans use.

1.

2.

3.

4.

B. Read the following passage.

AMERICAN OCCUPATIONS: PAST AND PRESENT

During the early colonization of the United States, most people were farmers. As the society became more industrialized, the number of necessary farmers drastically decreased, and many people moved to the larger, more urban areas of the country to find jobs. Because of new technology and industrialization, different types of occupations were developed.

With the shift from farming to industrialization, many blue-collar jobs were created. In January 1995, the U.S. Department of Labor reported that blue-collar jobs made up 25.5% of the workforce. This percentage, however, is rapidly decreasing because of the competition from imported products and the new technology that has replaced many jobs with computer-operated machinery.

Most blue-collar jobs require some kind of manual labor and can be divided into three different types: unskilled, semiskilled, and skilled labor. Unskilled jobs require little formal education; most of the necessary skills can be learned directly on the job. Examples of unskilled blue-collar jobs include washing dishes and cooking at a fast food restaurant. Semiskilled blue-collar workers often operate machines on assembly lines in large factories. These workers have received specific training for a specific skill such as automobile or electronic equipment assembly line work. Finally, skilled blue-collar work requires intense training in a specific trade. Most workers go through a training period, or apprenticeship. Plumbers, electricians, and other craftsworkers are all skilled workers who usually belong to unions that help protect them and regulate their work.

Just as industrialization created more blue-collar jobs, industrial technology also created white-collar occupations. White-collar jobs now make up 58.5% of the occupations in the United States as a result of the broad range of training, skills, and working environments that are involved. There are essentially two types of white-collar occupations. The first type concerns jobs that are based on the handling (producing, recording, classifying, and storing) of information. This type of white-collar occupation includes clerical (office), sales, managerial, or technical work. The second type includes the professionals, such as lawyers, doctors, teachers, and engineers, who usually have more specialized education backgrounds.

The third category of occupations is the fastest growing sector in the economy—service jobs. Service occupations are replacing many of the manufacturing jobs that have disappeared as a result of advanced technology. Service workers, who make up 13.3% of the labor force, provide some kind of service directly to individuals. Restaurant and hotel jobs are some of the more obvious service occupations. In addition, many small businesses and organizations in the United States provide services such as cleaning and repairing of various products. There are also many Americans who work privately in many different types of service jobs, such as home health-care aides, music teachers, etc.

Last, although it is the smallest sector of American jobs, farming occupations still exist. Only 2.7% of American workers are employed in agriculture, as farmers or farm laborers. This category also includes occupations in forestry, fishing, and mining.

Although classifying jobs in this manner is helpful when describing the different sectors of the American workforce, labels like blue-collar, white-collar, service, and farm are dangerously limiting. Individuals may possess skills that cross categories. Also, job requirements change as new technology is developed.

References

Economics Today and Tomorrow. Mission Hills, CA: Glencoe/McGraw Hill, 1991.

Rose, P., P. Glazer, and M. Glazer. *Sociology: Understanding Society.* Englewood Cliffs, NJ: Prentice-Hall, 1990.

United States, Department of Labor, Bureau of Labor Statistics, *Employment and Earnings.* Washington, D.C.: GPO, 1995.

C. Sometimes readers make outlines of a reading passage to understand it better. Fill in the missing parts in the outline for this passage on job classifications, using the diagram on pages 100–101. Some of the diagram has already been filled in for you.

Outlines

Outlines are visual tools that represent the relationship and importance of ideas. Outlines are useful when listening to a lecture or when taking notes on a reading. Look at the format of the accompanying blank diagram of an outline. When you write an outline, especially if your instructor asks you to turn one in, keep in mind some of these guidelines:
1. Place ideas of equal importance at corresponding levels. For example, all the main ideas of an outline should go under the roman numerals (I, II, III), the next important ideas should go under the capital letters (A, B, C), etc.
2. Move from the very general at the first level (roman numerals) to the more specific as you progress down the levels (capital letters, ordinal numbers, etc.). In other words, the items listed next to a capital letter or an ordinal number are the supporting details for the main idea listed next to the roman numeral.

   I. Industrialization of the United States
      A. More industrialization led to the decrease in farmers.
      B. People moved to urban areas and different occupations were developed.
  II. Blue-collar workers (25.5% of the workforce)
      A. Unskilled labor
         1. dishwashers
         2.
      B.
         1. assembly line workers (automobile)
         2. assembly line workers (electronic equipment)
      C. Skilled labor
         1.
         2.
         3. other craftsworkers

III.
    A. Information handlers
        1. sales workers
        2.
        3.
        4.
    B.
        1. lawyers
        2. doctors
        3.
        4.
IV. Service workers (13.3% of the workforce)
    A. Major service organizations
        1.
        2. restaurants
    B. Small businesses/organizations
        1.
        2. repairing
    C.
        1. home health-care aides
        2. music teachers
V. Farmers (2.7% of the workforce)
    A.
    B.
    C.
    D.

D. Categorize the different occupations into the proper categories. In order to figure out which occupation fits into each category, ask yourself how much training or skill is necessary to perform the job, how long it takes to acquire the skill, and where the job is performed. Some examples are given.

grocery bagger	professor	karate teacher
bus driver	beekeeper	computer programmer
machinist	accountant	musician
fire fighter	office manager	nurse

White-Collar	Blue-Collar	Service	Farm
physician	truck driver	police officer	farmer

E. On the left is a list of some sexist job titles. Can you unscramble the letters of the words in the right column to reveal the nonsexist alternatives?

Sexist Job Titles	Nonsexist Job Titles	
1. sound man	nsoud necthiiacn	_sound technician_
2. handyman	pshydanoner	_____
3. fireman	reif gfireht	_____
4. workman	rokwre	_____
5. chairman	pciesrharon	_____
6. mailman	aplost rrrciae	_____
7. stewardess	glithf tatenatnd	_____
8. policeman	lpioce fifcroe	_____
9. businessman	pbussseinenors	_____

F. Look at the list of subjects and occupations. Based on the number of syllables and the stress (see chapter 2), put the words in the appropriate place in the chart that follows. An example has been done for you.

economics   politics   history   psychologist
engineer   politician   economist   psychology
historian   mathematician   engineering   mathematics

Subject	Person
1. ☐☐■☐ economics	☐■☐☐ economist
2. ☐■☐☐	☐■☐☐
3. ☐☐■☐	☐☐■
4. ■☐☐	☐■☐☐
5. ■☐☐	☐☐■☐
6. ☐■☐	☐☐■☐

II. Earnings and Benefits

A. Get into groups and brainstorm the benefits that the different people might get in each occupation.

Occupation	Possible Benefits
Clothing store clerk	*free or discounted store merchandise*
College professor	
High school teacher	
Airplane mechanic	
Restaurant manager	
Book publisher	

B. Read the following passage.

EARNINGS AND BENEFITS FOR AMERICAN JOBS

The earnings and benefits a worker receives in the United States vary according to several different factors. In the United States, a person's earnings can be based on several different types of pay plans. Workers may be paid a straight annual salary (paid weekly, biweekly, or monthly), an hourly wage, commissions based on a percentage of what they sell, or a piece rate for each item they produce. Others receive tips for services to customers. Workers also may be paid a combination of a salary plus commission, or a salary or hourly wage plus bonus or tips.

Many workers receive employer-paid benefits in addition to wages and salaries. These are informally called "perks." Teachers, for example, get summers off; college faculty get sabbatical leave and tuition for dependents; pilots, flight attendants, and aircraft mechanics working for airlines get free or discounted air travel for themselves and their families; and retail sales workers get discounted merchandise.

Benefits can vary depending on where an employee works. Most state and local government employees, for example, generally have better medical and dental care, life insurance, retirement plans, and different types of leave than workers in the private sector.

Benefits can also vary with the size of the company. Workers employed in medium and large firms with 100 or more employees enjoy better benefits than workers in small firms with fewer than 100 workers. Medium and large firms generally provide better medical and dental insurance, life insurance, and retirement benefits, as well as longer unpaid maternity leave and long-term disability insurance. Unlike in most developed countries, maternity and paternity leave in the United States is often unpaid. Paid vacations and holidays and medical care and life insurance are generally the major benefits available to the majority of workers in small firms.

Finally, benefits vary depending on whether the work is full or part time. For example, one third of part-time employees received paid vacations and holidays in 1991, compared with over four-fifths of full-time workers. Most Americans do not enjoy very long vacations, however. Two weeks per year is the average length of vacation for most Americans, but the length of the vacation certainly depends on the length of employment and the size of the company. Most American employees have to work for a company longer than 10 years in order to receive more than two to three weeks of vacation.

In conclusion, earnings and benefits depend on where a person works, the size of the company, and whether or not the person works part time or full time.

References

Biracree, Tom, and Nancy Biracree. *Almanac of the American People.* New York: Facts on File, 1988, 161.

United States, Department of Labor, Bureau of Labor Statistics, *Occupational Outlook Handbook.* Bulletin 2450. Washington, D.C.: GPO, 1995.

C. Read the following statements. Write a *T* if the sentence is true or an *F* if the sentence is false.

1. ____ Employees of small firms usually have better benefits than those of larger firms.
2. ____ Most Americans have to work for a company for a year in order to get more than two or three weeks vacation.
3. ____ Retirement benefits are usually available to employees of medium and large companies.
4. ____ Maternity and paternity leave in the United States is always paid.
5. ____ Part-time employees usually receive benefits similar to those of full-time employees.

D. Some of the following words are taken from the reading on pages 104–5. Three of the words on each line are similar in meaning. Circle the word that *does not* belong. Then, explain why each circled word does not belong.

1. wages	salary	job	earnings
2. worker	employee	employer	laborer
3. vacation	leave	holiday	overtime
4. cheaper	discounted	expensive	reduced
5. instructors	professors	clerical staff	faculty
6. benefits	perks	advantages	payments

E. Look at the following graph and answer the questions below.

1. What is the subject of the graph?
2. What does the horizontal axis represent?
3. What does the vertical axis represent?
4. What conclusions can you draw from the graph?

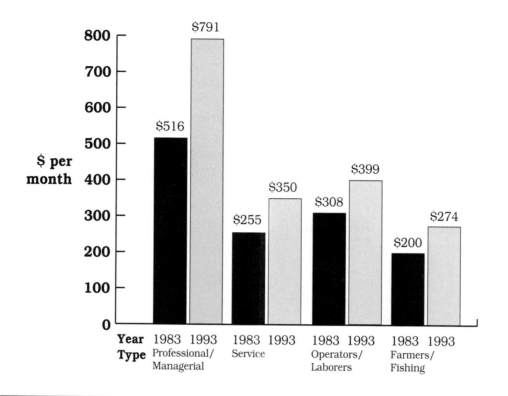

$ per month

Year	1983 1993	1983 1993	1983 1993	1983 1993
Type	Professional/ Managerial	Service	Operators/ Laborers	Farmers/ Fishing

Values shown: $516, $791, $255, $350, $308, $399, $200, $274

Interpreting Graphs

Many textbooks and readings use graphs to show patterns over a period of time. Writers use graphs to help readers fully understand information. Line and bar graphs are the most common types of graphs in American textbooks. These graphs usually show data that concerns two variables, one on a vertical line, the other along a horizontal line. Information is indicated either by dots connected with a line (line graph) or with solid bars (bar graph). It is important to understand the information in the graph, and it is also important to be able to explain that information. Following are some useful expressions to use:

This graph shows . . .
The subject of this graph is . . .
The horizontal axis represents . . .
The vertical axis represents . . .
The pattern revealed by this graph is . . .

Data for graph from United States, Bureau of Labor Statistics, *Bulletin 2307* and *Employment and Earnings Monthly*, January issue and United States, Department of Commerce, *Statistical Abstract of the United States* (Washington, D.C.: GPO, 1995).

F. Using the information regarding the average hours and earnings of blue-collar manufacturing workers, draw a bar graph. Do not forget to label your graph.

Year	Hourly Earnings
1970	$3.36
1975	$4.80
1980	$7.27
1985	$9.52
1990	$10.84

G. Scan the newspaper advertisements and write the names of the jobs in the appropriate place in the chart that follows.

Data for wages from United States, Bureau of Labor Statistics and *The 1994 Information Please Almanac* (Boston and New York: Houghton Mifflin, 1994).

800 General Help Wanted	Bridgeview Public Schools Hiring Bus Drivers for Fall!	**Restaurant Management** *New Market Expansion!*

800 General Help Wanted

Child care (afternoon only). Hickory Hills area, 3 girls, 6, 8, and 11. 20 hrs/wk., M-F. $9.50/hr.

Butterworth Healthcare
Home Health Aides
Up to $10/hr.

-Flexible hours
-Excellent Wages/Benefits

Call 555-2639

Service Tech for A/C & Heating. Apply at Champs Heating & Air Conditioning. Great wages and benefits. 64 W. Michigan Ave.

Bridgeview Public Schools Hiring Bus Drivers for Fall!

• paid training
• excellent salary, paid holidays, sick time, bonus, benefits
• off summers, winter and spring break
• must have good driving record

Bridgeview Public Schools is an Equal Opportunity / Affirmative Action Employer

Pizza Delivery Person needed. Friday and Saturday nights only. Must have own car. $5.00/hr. Free pizza.

Restaurant Management
New Market Expansion!

We're seeking managers for both Chicago and New York locations.

• attractive salaries
• excellent benefits
• promotion opportunities
• 5 day work week

Teacher's Aide for Wilkins Junior High School 7th grade program. Mornings only. $7.75/hr. M, W, F only. Come to the school office between 1-4 on Friday, 8/4.

Jobs Paying an Hourly Wage	Jobs Paying a Salary	Jobs with Benefits (type of benefit, if specified)
Home health aide		

Activity adapted from Barry Tomalin and Susan Stempleski, *Cultural Awareness* (Hong Kong: Oxford University Press, 1993), 65–68.

III. How Americans Work

A. The following list of words and phrases comes from the newspaper article on page 110. Which are associated with cooperation and which are associated with competition? Write them in the appropriate column of the chart that follows.

teamwork
sharing information
leading man or woman
what is this going to do
  for me?

individualism
capture the limelight
collaboration
"I" must be replaced
  with "we"

self-centered
soloist
"me" culture
trust

Cooperation	Competition

B. Before reading the following newspaper article carefully, preview the article by looking at the title, subtitles, pictures, and picture captions. Write down any words or phrases in the space that follows that represent what the text will be about.

Ryan Morrish takes part in a quality control check as part of A.B. Heller's training in blueprint reading. The Milford firm helps employees develop relationships with others while learning how their jobs fit into the big picture.

More firms replacing 'I' with 'We' in a bid to overcome the cultural barriers created by individualism, technology

Making teamwork work

By Angelo B. Henderson
The Detroit News

To promote teamwork, a Milford-based manufacturing firm launched a classroom program to teach employees how to listen and communicate better.

After five months of hearing plant workers grumble *"what is this going to do for me?"*, the classes at A.B. Heller Inc. were canceled.

"What I couldn't understand was how they could sit at home the night before watching the best team win a game on TV, and then wonder why they needed to be a team at work," said Peter Rosenkrands, president of Heller, which produces diesel-injection systems.

Quickly, Rosenkrands learned that it takes more than classes to change the way employees think about teamwork — especially when American culture praises individualism.

"In this country, we are really motivated toward individual achievement and individual excellence," said Marietta Baba, professor of anthropology at Wayne State University.

And it's that self-centered mentality among American employees that's making it harder for U.S. companies to implement new ideas, develop more efficient processes and apply better technology to compete globally, she said. Baba speaks with authority. For the last five years, she has studied how cultural barriers hinder change in the workplace.

One result was "The Cultural Dimensions of Technology-Enabled Corporate Transformation," a report compiled by Baba; Donald Falkenburg, professor and chairman of industrial and manufacturing engineering at Wayne State University; and David Hill, a former chief information officer of General Motors Corp.

The study was based on more than 500 interviews at all levels of operations in various automotive and aerospace companies undergoing new projects and programs.

The research added proof to the notion that what people think often is influenced by what they have experienced. And in America, the axiom is "Look out for No. 1."

From kindergarten through college, students are discouraged from sharing information or ideas — that's often considered cheating.

Typically, children are taught to find out what they do well, excel and compete against their peers, and be No. 1.

Often, it is one high achiever who captures the limelight, gaining more recognition than the entire group that made the task possible.

In a choir, it's the soloist. In a movie, it's the leading man or woman. In the operating room, it's the surgeon.

Likewise, in the corporate ranks, an employee is usually reviewed and evaluated individually, just like a cake in a bake-off at the state fair.

"We think competition among individuals brings out the best in people, but it also keeps people from cooperating," Baba said.

Photos by Alan Lessig / The Detroit News

Instructor Doug Krzyaniak gives assistance to worker Bryan Spaller. While teamwork classes failed at A.B. Heller in Milford, voluntary classes teaching specific skills, including blueprint reading, have been a big success.

And that *"me"* culture in companies becomes *"my department," "my group," "my division,"* she said.

"In the traditional organization, the creative people develop a design and throw it over the walls to the engineers, who will do development and testing and throw it over the walls to the manufacturing people," Baba said.

"Problems are created when work groups don't cooperate. It's a much more expensive process because problems aren't detected early; work has to go back, and it becomes time consuming. A lot of quality problems can come about, resulting in higher costs."

The message is clear: cooperation, collaboration and trust. "I" must be replaced by "We."

Sean Mayer solves a problem as instructor Doug Krzyaniak observes during a blueprint reading class for employees of A.B. Heller Inc. in Milford.

From the *Detroit News*, September 5, 1994, "Discovery" section.

C. Match the following words to their definitions by writing the correct letter in the blank space.

_____ 1. implement   a. working together or with someone

_____ 2. hinder   b. discovered; found

_____ 3. notion   c. experiencing

_____ 4. collaboration   d. to put into practice

_____ 5. detected   e. idea; opinion

_____ 6. grumble   f. to prevent

_____ 7. promote   g. to complain or protest

_____ 8. axiom   h. statement that is accepted as true

_____ 9. undergoing   i. becomes the center of attention

_____ 10. captures the limelight j. help to organize and start

D. Answer the following questions based on the newspaper article.

1. Why are students discouraged from sharing information or ideas in American schools?

2. According to Marietta Baba, what are one positive and one negative aspect of competition?

3. What problems are created when work groups do not cooperate?

4. What has the American self-centered attitude made it harder for companies to do?

E. Get into groups and decide what some effective ways might be to improve cooperation in the American workplace.

F. Just as the idea of competition and cooperation might differ between Americans and other cultures, the different perceptions of time are also an issue. Get into small groups and look at each of the different appointments listed in the following chart. Discuss what time you would arrive for each one in your country and then decide as a group what time an American would probably arrive. Are there differences between you and other people in your group or you and Americans? How are these times different and why?

Appointments	You	American
1. 1:00 P.M. job interview at a bank		
2. 12:30 P.M. business lunch date		
3. 7:00 P.M. dinner date with your boyfriend or girlfriend at a restaurant		
4. Consecutive meetings at 1:00 P.M. and 2:00 P.M.		
5. 8:00 A.M. business meeting		
6. 9:00 P.M. party at a colleague's home		

IV. Values Application

A. Read the following statements. Which one do you think is a fact and which is an opinion?

1. It's easy to get a service job in health care in the United States.
2. The service-producing industry is the fastest growing industry in the United States.

Distinguishing between Fact and Opinion

Whenever you are reading, especially when you are reading about a controversial issue, it is important that you are able to distinguish between statements of fact and statements of opinion.

Facts are statements that can be proven true or false with evidence that is unbiased (someone's personal opinion).

Opinions can also be valid statements, even based on experience or research, but they usually express a personal point of view. Opinions cannot be proven with unbiased evidence.

It's not always easy to differentiate between a fact and an opinion because some statements present statistics to make them appear like facts although a personal point of view is still expressed.

B. Read the following statements regarding trends in the job market at the end of the century. Mark "O" for any statement you believe is an opinion or interpretation of the facts. Mark "F" for any statement you believe is a fact. Mark "I" for any statement you think is impossible to judge.

1. _____ Half-hour lunches in the United States are too short.

2. _____ Women are much more cooperative workers than men.

3. _____ According to a survey by DayTimers Inc., specialists in time management, the average American worker spends 6 hours per week working at home on job-related material.

4. _____ The number of women in the workforce has increased 44% since 1960.

5. _____ The American view of competition vs. cooperation will lead to a failure in the U.S. economy.

6. _____ The average paid lunch hour in the United States is 27 minutes.

7. _____ The number of Americans who are self-employed continues to rise.

C. Look at the sentences in Activity B that describe several aspects of the American workplace. What values (see p. 17) do you think are reflected in each sentence?

Chapter 6

Getting Along: Family Life in the United States

Imagine that these pictures are from various family albums. What types of families do these pictures represent? Which ones do you think are the most common in the United States?

A Look Behind/A Look Ahead

In the last chapter we studied various aspects of the American workplace. We learned that occupations are classified into four categories: blue collar, white collar, service, and farm jobs. We also learned about earnings and benefits of several American jobs. In addition, we explored several American values. In this chapter, we are going to look closely at the American family—its structure, the changes in this structure, the older generation, and the values associated with American family life.

To the Student

After completing this chapter, you will be able to

1. differentiate between nuclear and extended families;
2. recognize the changes in American families;
3. argue for and against working mothers;
4. understand the older generation's need for independence in the United States.

Vocabulary Development

Throughout this book, we have learned about the pronunciation and grammar (i.e., the part of speech) of words in English. In addition, we have learned certain strategies for guessing the meaning of words we don't know, by looking at the word's morphology and the surrounding context. We have also studied how to use a dictionary to discover more about the pronunciation, grammar, and meanings of vocabulary words.

You have been introduced to many new vocabulary words in this textbook. What is the best way to remember all of these new words? Well, researchers in second language acquisition believe that people will remember vocabulary better if it is presented in a contextualized and meaningful way and if it is recycled, or reused, again and again. All of the vocabulary that you learned in this text was essential for understanding the larger picture of culture, and most of the important words were recycled throughout the chapters. This method of presentation should help you retain the new words that you learned in this book, but you will also probably need to do some extra studying of any new vocabulary words. Making and studying vocabulary cards are useful tools to help you remember words. Look at this example of a vocabulary card.

---

norm (n) standard example of behavior; that which is regarded as average or acceptable; normal (adj); normalize (v); normally (adv)

Dual-career families have become the *norm* rather than the exception.

You do not need to follow the format of this card exactly; write out the information about a vocabulary word in a way that is helpful to you. It is very important, however, that you use the vocabulary word in a sentence that makes sense to you. Study these vocabulary cards whenever you have any free time: riding on a bus, waiting for an appointment, or just before you go to sleep. As you encounter new words that are important to you in this chapter, make vocabulary cards for these words and study them often.

I. Family Structures

A. Many families in the United States are considered "nuclear" families. The general definition of nuclear families is families in which there are a mother, father, and children living in one house. "Extended" families, on the other hand, usually consist of grandparents, aunts, uncles, or cousins living in one house. Listen to the following people describe their families. Decide whether each person comes from a nuclear family or an extended family. Write "N" for nuclear and "E" for extended.

1. ____

2. ____

3. ____

Now write some of the characteristics that you heard about nuclear families and extended families.

Nuclear Families	*Extended Families*

B. Get into groups and fill in the following chart with advantages and disadvantages of both nuclear and extended families.

	Advantages	*Disadvantages*
Nuclear Families		
Extended Families		

II. Changing Family Structures

A. Read this quote and answer the questions that follow.

Conflict and change are inherent in social life. If the family is now in a state of flux, such is the nature of resilient* institutions; if it is beset* by problems, so is life. The family will survive.
—Arlene Skolnick, "The Paradox of Perfection," 1980

What does *inherent* mean? What do you think this quote means? What types of changes and/or problems do you think the American family has experienced?

_____

resilient strong enough to recover; *beset* troubled.

B. Quickly skim through the following passage, "American Families of the '90s," by reading the first sentence of each paragraph and by looking at any words that are printed in italics, any charts, and any pictures. Without looking back at the passage, write down some of the main ideas.

C. Now, read the entire passage. As you read it, underline any vocabulary words you don't know. *Do not* look them up in a dictionary; simply underline them.

AMERICAN FAMILIES OF THE '90S

The structure of the American family has changed considerably in the second half of the 20th century. A *family* is still idealized as a married couple with the husband as breadwinner, the wife as homemaker, and all the children living under one roof until they get married or move out on their own. Today, only one in four of all families fits this model of a nuclear family. The American Home Economics Association has defined the family as "two or more persons who share resources, share responsibility for decisions, share values and goals, and have commitments to one another over a period of time." We also have to consider the United States Bureau of the Census's definition of a *household* (all the people living in a house), which includes single people and nonfamilies (unrelated people, childless couples, homosexual couples, etc). As you see, these definitions allow for many different forms of a family.

One reason that families have changed is due to the continuous increase in the number of divorces among Americans. The United States has the highest divorce rate in the world. Over one million divorces occur each year in the country (half of them within the first seven years of marriage), and it is predicted that over 60% of the children born during the 1980s can expect their parents to divorce or separate at some point. The increased divorce rate is the result of several changes in the United States. Women have experienced an increase in financial and social independence; the deindustrialization of the United States has made the employment of women necessary; and the public, legal, and religious attitudes toward divorce have changed toward greater acceptance.

Another reason the traditional idea of the family has changed is due to the trend toward independent living for both the younger and older generations. More and more adults are remaining single, living together without getting married, waiting longer to get married, delaying having children, or not having children at all. The average age for marriage in the United States has increased to 26.5

% of population living alone

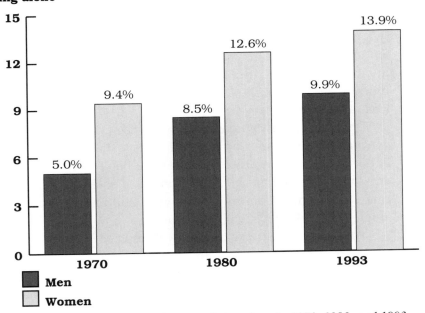

Percentage of men and women living alone in 1970, 1980, and 1993.

for men and 24.5 for women from 23.2 and 20.8 in 1970. Many young adults move out of their parents' home, establish their own households, and attend college or start a career before getting married. This attitude toward marriage and the fact that more women are seeking further education and career opportunities has resulted in more couples than ever before deciding not to have children at all.

Data from United States, Bureau of the Census, Department of Commerce, *Statistical Abstract of the United States 1994*, 114th ed. (Washington, D.C.; GPO, 1994).

One last reason for the change away from the traditional family is the economic situation of families and the whole country. Although many mothers have left the home to pursue career or educational goals, some have been forced out into the workforce even though they may not have desired to be employed for pay. This has altered the traditional composition of the family with the mother as homemaker and main child care provider. Also, although some women have chosen to work, the continual increase in the cost of living and the rise in costs of higher education have made working outside the home a necessity rather than a choice.

What has happened as a result of these changes? In the most general sense, family structures that were not considered traditional in the past are now accepted as the norm. For example, blended families (consisting of remarried couples and their children from previous marriage) occur more and more often. Adoptive families, foster families, interracial families, married couples without children, and homosexual families also exist more frequently today than they ever did in the past. The most common types of families in the United States include single-parent, childless, and, finally, two-worker families.

Because of the rising number of divorces, single-parent homes continue to increase. Some people believe that the rise in the number of one-parent families indicates the deterioration of the American family as well as the deterioration of society. Whether or not this is true, projections into the year 2000 show that the rise of single-parent families will continue.

Today, nearly 30% of all family groups with children are maintained by single parents. This is a major increase from 12% in 1970. The majority of these single-parent families are headed by women. Some of these families (20%) are headed by a mother who has never married. One less parent in the home can cause financial problems, especially for single mothers. The cost of child care causes an additional financial burden.

Another large group of households in the United States is single adults, nonfamily households, and childless couples. Over the past two decades, the number of women living alone rose 94% (7.3 million to 14.2 million) and the number of men living alone rose 167% (3.5 million to 9.4 million). This includes both young and older single people. Then there are more nonfamily households: unmarried, homosexual, and unrelated people living together. For example, 86% more men and women cohabited without getting married in 1993 than in 1970. Sociologists have labeled this type of couple *POSSLQs* (persons of opposite sex sharing living quarters). In addition, the proportion of married couples without children exceeds the number of married couples with children. The sociological label for dual-earner couples without children is *DINK* (double-income, no kids).

The last common type of family is the dual-career family. As you can probably guess, the reasons for this change are economic and social. There have been an unprecedented number of women entering the workforce during this century. Those with children usually have more money to spend on their children, but they certainly have less time. This change has had various effects on society's perception of the family.

The effect that two working parents may have on the children of the family is a controversial issue. Some people believe that the family is weakened as a result of two working parents. They feel that the working parents do not spend enough time with the children. In addition, there is added stress and possible neglect to the children, which may eventually affect them and the society as a whole.

For many families it is financially necessary for both parents to work, and some people believe that there are positive effects. For example, work often fulfills a psychological need for the parents. If the parents are more content with their lives, the family environment will be more peaceful. Also, two incomes lessen the money problems that a one breadwinner household might have, which would have a more positive effect on the children.

As we have seen, the increase in the proportions of single, unmarried couple, and single-parent households has forced a change in the traditional perception of the nuclear family. The family is still one of the most idealized institutions in the United States, and the changes that have occurred, especially during the second half of this century, are under constant scrutiny because of the disruption that some of these changes have seemed to cause. However, it does seem that Americans are moving away from emphasizing one specific type of family and have begun to accept many different types.

References

Bender, David L., and Bruno Leone, eds., *Family in America.* San Diego: Greenhaven Press, 1992.

Masnick, George, and Mary Jo Bane. *The Nation's Families: 1960–1990.* Boston: Auburn House Publishing Company, 1980.

Roberts, Sam. *Who We Are: A Portrait of America.* New York: Times Books, 1993.

Spies, Karen B. *The American Family: Can It Survive?* New York: Twenty-First Century Books, 1993.

United States, Bureau of the Census, *Statistical Abstract of the United States: 1994.* 114th ed. (Washington, D.C.: GPO, 1994).

The World Almanac and Book of Facts. Mahwah, N.J.: Funk and Wagnalls Corp., 1994.

D. Answer the following questions about the organization of the passage.

1. What paragraph serves as the introduction to the passage?

2. What are the three causes for the changes in the American family mentioned in the passage? What support does the writer use for these ideas?

3. What is the second issue discussed in the passage?

4. What are the three examples the writer provides? What support does the writer use for these examples?

5. What paragraph serves as the conclusion for the passage?

E. Write the sentences that express each main idea in the reading passage.

F. Choose some of the words in the passage that you underlined in Activity C. First, write the sentence that contains the vocabulary word. Next, decide which strategy you will use for that vocabulary word from the guidelines in the language box on this page. If you cannot ignore the word, write the definition in the space provided. Two examples have been done for you.

Summary of Vocabulary Strategies

The following strategies can be used when you are confronted with a vocabulary word you do not know:

1. ignore the word;
2. guess the meaning from the surrounding context;
3. guess the meaning from the word's morphology;
4. use a dictionary.

Always begin with number 1. If you can ignore the word, then do so. If the word, however, is necessary to understand the meaning of the sentence, then use one or more of the remaining strategies. Try to become less dependent on your dictionary, as constantly looking up words slows your reading down.

Example:

> For example, 86% more men and women *cohabited* without getting married in 1993 than in 1970.
>
> *Strategy:* 3—I can guess this word from the morphology. I know that *co* means "together," and I guessed that *habit* means "live."
>
> *Definition:* to live together

> For example, *blended families* (consisting of remarried couples and their children from previous marriage) occur more and more often.
>
> *Strategy:* 2—guess from surrounding context
>
> *Definition:* consisting of remarried couples and their children from previous marriage

1. _____

   _____

   Strategy:

   Definition:

2. _____

   _____

   Strategy:

   Definition:

3. _____

   _____

   Strategy:

   Definition:

4. _____

_____

Strategy:

Definition:

5. _____

_____

Strategy:

Definition:

6. _____

_____

Strategy:

Definition:

G. Listen to the introduction of a radio talk show interview about different work and family roles. Under each couple's names, fill in the different work and family situation that each one has (dual-career family, stay at home father, stay at home mother). Ignore the rest of the chart right now.

Couples / Situations	Arguments for	Arguments against
Sabine and Stephan Helling *Situation:*		
Ann and Sam Wurster *Situation:*		
Scott and Andrea Borden *Situation:*		

H. Listen to the whole interview and fill in the chart in Activity G with the arguments for and against the three different work and family situations.

I. Below is a list of counterarguments, arguments against dual-career marriages. Read the arguments and write a statement that refutes the argument, or shows that the argument is incorrect. Use the information from the reading passage in Activity C and the talk show interview in Activity G.

1. *Argument:* When both parents work, they spend less time with their children.
   Refutation:

2. *Argument:* If both parents have careers, there will be more stress on the whole family.
   Refutation:

J. Do you think that dual-career families are positive or negative? Choose a side and write an argumentative essay on a separate sheet of paper.

Argumentative Essays

The following provides a possible organizational plan for an argumentative essay.

   I. Introduction
  II. Background paragraph about the topic
 III. Pro argument 1*
 IV. Pro argument 2
  V. Pro argument 3
 VI. Counterarguments and refutations
VII. Conclusion

III. The Older Generation

A. Scan the following reading passage and find a word(s) in each corresponding line that best fits the given meaning.

1. (2)   Which word(s) means *separation from others?*
2. (2)   Which word(s) means *shocking?*
3. (10) Which word(s) means *a heavy duty or responsibility?*

---

*Some writers think it is better to put your weakest argument first and build to your strongest argument.

4. (12) Which word(s) means *continue?*
5. (13) Which word(s) means *to involve or make necessary?*
6. (15) Which word(s) means *important?*
7. (17) Which word(s) means *the quality or manner of a person's life?*
8. (23) Which word(s) means *giving or allowing?*
9. (23) Which word(s) means *independence?*

B. Read the following passage.

ANY ROOF BUT THE KIDS'

Old people tend to spend their days among other old people—or alone. The isolation of the old is astounding to newcomers to the United States. Traditional cultures would never think up such a thing as an old-age home, an establishment made up entirely of
5   unrelated old people and their caretakers.

However, you should not assume that old people are rejected because they're isolated. Whether or not the relationship is a happy one, grown children feel responsible for the care of aging parents (or at least for seeing they get care). But independence is valued as
10 much by the old as it is by the young. "I never want to be a burden on my children," is a common phrase on the lips of parents.

Better to keep on in your own home, with all the effort and expense that entails. "Alone" may mean "lonely," but being lonely is better than loss of freedom. Many old people do have nearby
15 relatives who help out, but the critical point is to remain in one's own home.

Even an old-age home is not always considered such a bad lot. Some are awful, but others are gracious and elegant—and expensive. Paying guests know that they are at least of financial worth
20 to the institution, which is better than being a family dependent.

The children may even be financing their parents' stay in the institution, but by not having them under their own roof they are graciously according them some remaining autonomy. Just as their parents encouraged them to be independent at a young age, the
25 children are now allowing the parents to be independent.

Information from Esther Wanning, *Culture Shock! USA* (Portland: Graphic Arts Center Publishing Company, 1991).

C. List the advantages and disadvantages of living in an old-age home that were described in the reading. Add any more that you think of to the lists.

IV. Values Application

A. Read each of the statements that describe aspects of American families. Choose the American value(s) each one represents among the values that we talked about in chapter 1.

Statement	Value(s)
1. A boy and his two sisters each have their own room.	
2. A 13-year-old daughter is the only vegetarian in the family, so she cooks a different meal from her family's almost every night.	
3. Both the mother and father of a family of five work, but they take turns cooking and cleaning.	
4. Each family member has certain jobs around the house to take care of every week.	
5. A grandfather moved into a retirement home after his wife died, even though his two sons live in the same city as he does.	
6. A 10-year-old child is given the choice to live with either his recently divorced mother or father.	